# SOME MYTHICAL ELEMENTS IN
# ENGLISH LITERATURE

# Some Mythical Elements in English Literature

BEING THE CLARK LECTURES 1959-60

E.M.W. TILLYARD

LITT.D., F.B.A.

1961

CHATTO & WINDUS

LONDON

Published by
Chatto & Windus Ltd
42 William IV Street
London WC2
*
Clarke, Irwin & Co. Ltd
Toronto

PRINTED IN GREAT BRITAIN BY
T. & A. CONSTABLE LTD, EDINBURGH

# CONTENTS

PREFACE                                          *page* 7

I. INTRODUCTION                                         9
   1. What is a Myth?                                   9
   2. Myth and Literature                              13
   3. Method of Treatment                              18

II. THE HARROWING OF HELL                              19
   1. Preface                                          19
   2. Origin of the Myth                               20
   3. The Reason for the Myth's Vogue                  23
   4. The Harrowing of Hell in Medieval Literature     31

III. TWO TUDOR MYTHS                                   45
   1. Preface                                          45
   2. The Myth of Pedigree                             46
   3. The Myth of Divine Appointment                   53

IV. AGGRESSION                                         66

V. RETIREMENT                                          72
   1. The Initial Phase                                72
   2. Transitional Phase                               84
   3. Climax                                           91
   4. Retrospect                                      102

VI. LIBERTY, OR 1066 AND ALL THAT                     108

INDEX                                                 139

# PREFACE

First, I must express my sincere thanks to the Master and Fellows of Trinity College, Cambridge, for inviting me to give the Clark Lectures for the year 1959-60. And I am indebted to the invitation not only for the high honour it does me but for its having propelled me to develop and express ideas that had been hovering in my mind for some time.

The resultant lectures are printed as delivered. They aim at being suggestive over a wide area, not at being thorough; and by preserving the lecture-form I hope to keep that aim before the reader's attention.

The translation of the Chinese poem on page 14 is reprinted by kind permission of the Cambridge University Press. It comes from *Chinese Lyrics* translated by Ch'u Ta-Kao (1937), and its original is by Fan Chung-Yen, who lived A.D. 989-1053.

I have to thank Professor E. M. Wilson for information about the Council of Trent's action against the *Gospel of Nicodemus*.

E. M. W. T.

# I. INTRODUCTION

## 1. *What is a Myth?*

I MUST first of all apologise for the extreme dimness of my title. The words *myth*, *mythical*, *mythology*, *mythological* have been dreadfully overworked in recent years and have a distressingly large range of significances. I would have avoided them if I could; but there exist no synonyms for these words in the one out of the many possible senses in which I shall use them.

To make my intention clearer let me first dispose of certain meanings my title *could* bear and which it emphatically does not.

You might have guessed from it that *mythical* meant imagined or non-existent and that I proposed to discuss certain supposed parts of literature, such as the different literary kinds or the intrinsic sonal value of words or phrases, and to show that they were chimerical.

Or you might have guessed that I was using myth in the sense of folklore and legend and that I intended to deal with the Prometheus myth or the Orpheus myth or the Arthur myth, and the uses to which this or that writer or epoch put them.

Or you might have guessed I was using *mythical* in the sense more commonly expressed by archetypal, that I was to exploit themes dear to Gilbert Murray and Maud Bodkin: that I was going to inquire what use English writers have made of such recurrent, primordial figures as the Strong Man (Hercules or Samson) or of the Vamp

Woman (Helen or Cleopatra) or of the Bogey Man, traitor or enemy (Judas, Machiavelli, Cromwell, Napoleon).

No; when I use *myth*, *mythical*, I have none of the above uses in mind, but I refer to the universal instinct of any human group, large or small, to invest, almost always unconsciously, certain stories or events or places or persons, real or fictional, with an uncommon significance; to turn them into instinctive centres of reference; to make among stories A, B, C, D, all roughly having the same theme or moral, *one*, and one only, the type. Made thus typical, the story becomes a communal possession, the agreed and classic embodiment of some way of thinking or feeling.

In this sense the myth-making instinct is widespread. For instance, any lively and sizable family creates its own family myths. Schools have their mythology, and I will give you a simple example of myth-creation in my preparatory school. The headmaster, who might well have modelled himself on the corresponding character in Anstey's *Vice Versa*, had a strong sense of drama both in teaching and in chastising. When you began Latin, you were made to feel (and you welcomed the compulsion) that the grammar of the language extended in length, that it was an august pilgrimage, august but beset with perils, which you were privileged to enter on. The parts of that grammar, too, were invested with solemn significance. Take the declensions. The first two were initiatory, being comparatively simple, and they led on to the myth of that Hill of Difficulty, the Third Declension. I still remember my excitement when, miserable weakling though I was, I was allowed to proceed to it, to begin mounting that eminence. Or take something quite recent, the myth of St Paul's Cathedral during the Second World War. In view of the devastation near by, it was in itself remarkable that St Paul's was almost spared. But this escape became much more than its unrelated self. It became for the Londoner the myth of present endurance and of ultimate escape: so long as Wren's dome was intact, nothing could really go wrong. To feel the truth of this assertion, you have only to think how little it applied to Westminster Abbey. To enlarge from a cathedral to a whole town, think of the significance of Wigan (as against Runcorn or Middlesbrough for instance) as a mythical centre of reference for certain feelings, correct or not, about nineteenth-century industrialism.

Then there are the mythical figures. Some ten years ago Vicky, the cartoonist, showed he had a proper sense of these. In one of his pictures he drew a gigantic figure of John Bull, crossed it out, and drew facing him, a smaller starved figure in working dress, backed by a wall, holding a roll of cloth under his arm and a cricket bat in one hand, and labelled Percy Vere. Rubrics pointing to different parts of his body or of its setting read thus: WALL, to keep his back to; UPPER LIP, to keep stiff; NOSE, to put to the grindstone; CHIN, to take it on; CLOTH, to cut his coat according to; SOCKS, to pull up; STRAIGHT BAT, to play with on a sticky wicket. Vicky was right: in recognising John Bull as a piece of English mythology and in asserting that he was out of date.

Passing to events or stories, one can cite the historical event of the Spartans resisting the Persians at Thermopylae as the myth common to the western world of heroic courage against desperate odds, and the story of Romeo and Juliet as that of young love ending in tragedy.

Or take this account of the mythical value of the defeat of the Spanish Armada; it is the last paragraph of Garrett Mattingley's recent book on that event:

*Meanwhile, as the episode of the Armada receded into the past, it influenced history in another way. Its story, magnified and distorted by a golden mist, became a heroic apologue of the defence of freedom against tyranny, an eternal myth of the victory of the weak over the strong, of the triumph of David over Goliath. It raised men's hearts in dark hours and led them to say to one another: "What we have done once, we can do again." In so far as it did this the legend of the defeat of the Spanish Armada became as important as the actual event—perhaps more important.*

The most prominent myths belong to large groups and especially to nations. Here we find these centres of instinctive reference, these myths, becoming frighteningly important: how important, citizens of countries old in culture and rich in mythology often find difficult to grasp. It was one of the triumphs of the newly formed United States of America that they so quickly mythologised part of the events that led to their independence. Even so, they could not claim a mythology as rich as that of France or China for instance; and I have been wondering these last years what parts of the Second World War they would use to eke out their older stock. My curiosity was partly satsfied when I recently heard an American lecturer speak in a quite taken-for-granted way of "Marathon or the Battle of the Bulge". Nazi Germany provided a good example of how indispensable a national myth can be. One of the German myths is the Rhine; and an important element of the myth is Heine's poem on it, *Die Lorelei*. But

Heine was a Jew, and his poem was inadmissible. Yet the Nazis could not do without it, and it appeared in their school-books as being by an unknown author. We may be certain that in the infant Republic of Cyprus there is already a mythology based on the Cypriots' years of resistance; and perhaps we may be a little less disgusted at the Monkhouse Museum at Suez if we recognise how desperate is the need for myth in new nations.

Great political movements, too, need their mythology. One of the best known of these is the classless society of the Communists. And one of the most illuminating accounts of a myth in the sense in which I now use the word can be found in Georges Sorel's *Reflexions on Violence*, where he sees the General Strike not as a likely event but as an ideal centre of reference.

## 2. *Myth and Literature*

I hope I have now made the meaning of *mythical* in the present context clear enough for me to be able to go on to the relation of myth to literature. Much literature bears no relation, owing nothing to a specific group and being either personal or in its universality missing the group and reaching humanity at large. Let me give an example, on the principle of defining a thing by pointing to its contrary. One from a distant literature should be especially apt, for, if it touches us as nearly as something of our own, its chances of genuine universality are very high. This is a translation of a Chinese poem by Fan Chung-Yen about garrison duty, first in autumn, then in winter, on the distant frontier with Tartary. In the translation it is headed *On the Frontier*.

1    *All aspects change on the frontier when autumn comes:*
     *Wild geese fly southward without faltering;*
     *Shouts echo on all sides along the border when the bugle*
     *     blows;*
     *Amid a thousand mountains,*
     *In the spreading mists and the westering sun, the lonely*
     *     citadel is closed.*

2    *A cup of poor wine—my native land is ten thousand*
     *     miles away;*
     *The Huns have not yet been conquered; I have no power to*
     *     go home.*
     *The Tartar flute comes wailing over a land frost-bound;*
     *One can hardly sleep.*
     *The General's white hair and the soldiers' tears.*

If there is something Chinese about the terseness of presentation, about the simple and suggestive juxtapositions, the sentiments presented and the imaginative force with which they are presented admit no national limit. Long exile from a place where a man thinks he belongs will engender the same kind of regret in all mankind. Any man, of whatever race, who has had experience of static warfare with comparatively peaceful stretches, will develop a curiosity about the fellows on the other side of the line, how they live and what they are thinking, and will respond to the poet's mention of the Tartar flute. The poet's cunning in bringing together the frozen ground and the sound of the flute, leaving us to imagine the unifying bridge—the simple truth that sound travels with special resonance in still cold weather over a hard frost-bound earth—displays what Coleridge called the esemplastic power of the imagination in a manner quite unconfined to any one place or country of the world. Again, the poet's restraint in not sentimentalising the contrast between the wild geese who can fly southward and the soldiers who are chained to the frontier, in merely giving the bare facts that the geese *do* fly south and that the speaker has no power to go home, is, we feel, artistically quite admirable. The total experience conveyed is at once intensely personal and yet universal in its comprehensibility. It evades the group. Also it in no wise incites to action. No one, on reading it, would think first of all that he had better try to evade military service or agitate for greater flexibility in the higher military command. Any action it promotes would be through generally awakening the imaginative sympathies of the reader.

All this is to demonstrate the kind of literature that is the remotest possible from the kind I shall treat of in these lectures.

Coming now to the literature I have in mind, I must make two obvious divisions. The first kind is literature that derives from and reinforces existing operant myth. I give no examples now, because most of the works I shall refer to in my lectures belong here. The second is literature that is itself mythical, literature that a group have decided is *their* mouthpiece, that stands as the accepted type of their own opinions and emotions. Such mythical literature is often at the mercy of chance. In potential mythical power a dozen pieces of literature may be equal; and it is chance, not intrinsic merit, that determines the choice. Let me illustrate by two examples. This is Blake's *Holy Thursday* from *Songs of Experience*, and it refers to the service held on that day for the orphaned charity-children of London:

*Is this a holy thing to see*
*In a rich and fruitful land,*
*Babes reduced to misery,*
*Fed with cold and usurous hand?*

*Is that trembling cry a song?*
*Can it be a song of joy?*
*And so many children poor?*
*It is a land of poverty!*

*And their sun does never shine,*
*And their fields are bleak and bare,*
*And their ways are filled with thorns:*
*It is eternal winter there.*

*For where-e'er the sun does shine,*
*And where-e'er the rain does fall,*
*Babe can never hunger there,*
*Nor poverty the mind appal.*

And alongside that set this passage from near the beginning of Dickens's *Oliver Twist*. Goaded by hunger the workhouse boys decide that one of their number must protest about their diet. They cast lots who it shall be; and Oliver is chosen.

*The evening arrived; the boys took their places. The master, in his cook's uniform, stationed himself at the copper; his pauper assistants ranged themselves behind him; the gruel was served out; and a long grace was said over the short commons. The gruel disappeared; the boys whispered each other and winked at Oliver; while his next neighbours nudged him. Child as he was, he was desperate with hunger and reckless with misery. He rose from the table; and advancing to the master, basin and spoon in hand, said, somewhat alarmed at his own temerity:*

*"Please, Sir, I want some more."*

*The master was a fat healthy man; but he turned very pale. He gazed in stupefied astonishment on the small rebel for some seconds and then clung for support to the copper. The assistants were paralysed with wonder; the boys with fear.*

*"What!" said the master at length in a faint voice.*

*"Please, Sir," replied Oliver, "I want some more."*

Different as those two pieces are in form, they make the same protest and are sufficiently striking in themselves to claim the notice of many people; both are potentially mythical. If I had to say which is the more striking, I should point to Blake's single line, "Fed with cold and usurous hand", as containing more explosive material than anything in Dickens's admirably animated prose. But Blake had to wait a hundred years before he attracted many readers, while Dickens wrote and published his piece in the full tide of popular enthusiasm that greeted the *Pickwick Papers*. Oliver Twist asking for more became quickly the rallying point for generous indignation at a social evil and ended by being part of Victorian mythology, a strong practical corroboration of the anger that had caused its advancement to mythical eminence.

If I had time I should gladly pursue the topic of literature that is in itself a part of operant mythology. I should like, for instance, to relate it to Matthew Arnold's attempt, so strongly condemned today, to make of poetry a substitute for religion, for it is this kind of poetry, and this kind only, that has the chance of influencing conduct after the manner of religion. And I should like to conjecture how far, in the modern world, where tradition and the cultural sway of the home count for much less and widespread education and mass entertainment for much more, group opinion could be shepherded into creating, out of any literature it enjoys, myths that would work actively for its benefit. But these things would require another set of lectures. And though I shall sometimes include literature that *is* mythical, my main topic will be literature that depends on myth, that sets it forth, that corroborates it, that is too loyal to it to desert, and then supplant, the thing from which it derives.

### 3. *Method of Treatment*

Having chosen an outsize topic, it would be ludicrous if I tried to treat it comprehensively in six lectures. So I shall work through samples, taking from different periods myths that have inspired a substantial body of literature. I shall also try to end my treatment of each myth by pointing to a literary masterpiece which it has, in part at least, inspired. After the eighteenth century, in a more complicated society, it is much more difficult to isolate myths and describe their effect on literature. It is probable that "self-help", for instance, was a Victorian myth; but I should find it difficult to say how it enters the major literature of the age. For the sake of clarity, therefore, I have kept off any works later than the eighteenth century.

## II. THE HARROWING OF HELL

### 1. Preface

I WILL begin my section on the Harrowing of Hell with asking you to recall a picture of it not many yards from where we now are. Imagine yourselves entering King's College Chapel, walking through the screen towards the altar as far as the steps, and then turning right. You will then be facing the south windows, with the second from the east in front of you. On the left bottom panel of this window is represented the entombment of Christ; and next to it, on the right, is its sequel. This right-hand panel is, pictorially, filled largely by a building in the Renaissance style, furnished with a small tower on the left and an arched door below. On the roof of the main building alongside of the tower is set a red beast's head with saucer eyes and an enormous mouth, with one devil in the aperture and another flying above, like wasps near their nest. This mouth is the entry into Hell proper, the abode of the devils. In the doorway of the building, which represents the department of Hell called Limbo, kneel a man and a woman; and behind them obtrude four or five heads of aged people and a pair of hands held up in prayer. On the left stands a towering and massive figure, wearing a mantle of royal red and holding in his left hand a tall staff topped with a cross. With his right hand he grasps the hand of the kneeling man as if to lift him up. Trampled on by his feet is the pair of gates that once closed the arched doorway of

Limbo. The total picture shows the first act of Christ after his death on the cross: that of leaving his body in the tomb, breaking Hell's gates, and haling out Adam, Eve and other patriarchs for transference to their new home in Paradise. This act was known as the harrowing or subduing of Hell. The King's window, in point of treatment, is normally representative of the differing versions of this not entirely canonical series of acts; aesthetically it is one of the most eminent. Immediately on the right, in the next window, is shown the Resurrection. What is so remarkable about the Harrowing of Hell window in its setting among the other windows is its clarity, its assurance; in these qualities equalling if not surpassing the neighbouring panel of the Resurrection.

I shall speak first of the origin of this great religious myth, next of why it had such a hold on the medieval imagination, and last of its entry into English medieval literature.

## 2. Origin of the Myth

The article in the Christian creed of Christ's descent into Hell derives from scattered passages of Scripture. But on the central part of the episode as represented in the window, Scripture is silent. It says nothing about Christ, in his descent to Hell, pulling Adam out of Limbo and releasing other Old Testament characters from it. For this central part medieval artists and poets went outside Scripture to the so-called *Gospel of Nicodemus*, itself an appendix of an apocryphal book called the *Acts of Pilate*. There are versions of this book in Greek, Coptic, and Latin; and translations of them are easily accessible in

Montague James's *Apocryphal New Testament*. The version that James calls Latin A is behind the typical English medieval renderings of the myth.

The story of the *Gospel of Nicodemus* is that, after Christ died on the cross and before his Resurrection, Adam and Eve and the other souls who were living in the darkness of Hell suddenly felt the warmth of the sun and saw the shining of a bright light. Whereupon Adam and the other patriarchs and John the Baptist rejoiced and began talking hopefully among themselves. Seth then recalled how, when his father Adam lay sick, he went to the gates of Paradise and begged the Archangel Michael for the oil of mercy with which to heal his father's body. Michael could not give it him, but added that the Son of God would give it after several thousand years had elapsed. All the patriarchs rejoiced at Seth's words, knowing that their deliverance now was near. There follows an agitated dialogue between Satan and Hell personified, for they know that some disaster threatens them. They are particularly agitated because it was but recently that they were deprived of Lazarus. As they are talking, there is heard a cry calling for the gates of Hell to open so that the King of Glory may enter. Satan and Hell determine to bar the gates still more strongly. Whereupon the patriarchs renew the cry to open the gates. The next cry is a climax and decides the issue; and here I quote from the text of the apocryphal Gospel:

> *And there came a great voice as of thunder saying: Remove, O princes, your gates, and be ye lift up ye doors of Hell and the King of Glory shall come in. And when Hell saw that they so cried out twice, he said, as if he knew it not: Who is the King*

*of Glory? And David answered Hell and said: The Lord strong and mighty, the Lord mighty in battle, He is the King of Glory. . . . And now, O thou most foul and stinking Hell, open thy gates that the King of Glory may come in. And as David spake thus unto Hell, the Lord of Majesty appeared in the form of a man and lightened the eternal darkness and brake the bonds that could not be loosed; and the succour of His everlasting might visited us that sat in the deep darkness of our transgressions and in the shadow of death of our sins.*

The powers of Hell then express their terror and quarrel among themselves, while Christ, taking Adam by the right hand, gathered his saints around him and made the sign of the Cross over them, and, still holding Adam by the hand, "went up out of Hell, and all the saints followed him". Finally, he delivered them all to the Archangel Michael to be housed in Paradise. Enoch, Elias, and the saved thief join them on their way there.

The substance of the *Gospel of Nicodemus* is as early as the second century though the Gospel itself may be two centuries later; and by the age of Constantine its central event, the haling of Adam from Hell by Christ, had become a subject for the artists. After the turn of the millennium it became excessively common, both in the Byzantine and the western artistic traditions. In Byzantine art the devils are absent, and Christ, holding Adam by the hand, tramples on the shattered gates of Hell, their bosses and nails and hinges scattered around. There are splendid renderings in, for instance, some of the Athos monasteries, in churches in Cyprus and Serbia, and in a more recondite place, the so-called Exultet Rolls from South Italy. The church ceremony beginning *Exultet jam angelica turba caelorum* took place on Easter Eve and includes a reference to the descent into Hell. The rolls, dating from the tenth to the twelfth centuries, give illustrations of the different parts of the ceremony. The illustrations are outline drawings reinforced by pigment, showing Byzantine influence but possessing a movement and an energy rare in Byzantine art: and some are of uncommon beauty. And when they are of the descent to Hell they follow not the ceremony they purport to illustrate but the *Gospel of Nicodemus*. The rolls are available through a splendidly illustrated volume published by the Princeton University Press and edited by Myrtilla Avery. In England an early version is a romanesque carving in the Canons' Vestry in Bristol Cathedral, in which Christ not only holds Adam by the hand but tramples on Satan. Later versions in the western tradition, for instance the picture by Fra Angelico in the Regia Galleria Antica e Moderna in Florence or Tintoretto's in the church of San Cassiano in Venice, usually add patriarchs and devils to the essential elements of Christ, Adam, and the shattered gates of Hell. The King's College window accords perfectly with the central western tradition.

### 3. *The Reason for the Myth's Vogue*

Why was it that from the very mixed contents of the apocryphal gospels the myth of Christ's pulling Adam out of Limbo should have stood out and taken on so high an importance in the Middle Ages? To answer this question we must recognise and apply certain trends of thought and feeling powerful at the time.

First, there is the peculiar medieval kind of ambition:

that of grasping and assimilating all reality. It is a quality that used to be attributed to the Renaissance as against the Middle Ages; and indeed the men who forgot Greek and curtailed the range of things in many other ways might in the first instance be regarded as utterly disqualified in their aims. Nevertheless, if you are willing to allow for much initial curtailment you must admit that medieval aims were immense. Consider the cathedrals, the encyclopedias, the works of Aquinas, the *Divine Comedy*. All these are conspicuous in their desire to include. And inclusion can bear a double sense: the act of ranging wide, of gathering all types of things in the net, and the act of multiplying detail within the types. Dante in his poem gives equal attention to all parts of the universe and strengthens all his types of action and feeling with abundant examples.

But, secondly, mere abundance was not enough. To make sense of the universe you had to connect one item with another. Indeed, the passion to do so was so strong as to be to a modern quite fantastic. It will be less so if he thinks of pioneers in a new country wanting to bring all its parts within their ken and most of them under control and cultivation. King's College Chapel can again provide an apt illustration. Immediately above the window showing the escape of Adam, Eve, and the patriarchs from Hell is a window showing the escape of the Jews from their Egyptian captivity; and the reason for this siting is that one incident is regarded as the duplicate of the other. Indeed, there is more than mere duplication, for the Old Testament event was thought to presage the Harrowing of Hell, which in its turn fulfilled the prophecy. Thus concatenated, the two events were brought within the scope of the reason. The whole series of windows in King's Chapel is arranged according to this duplication or fulfilment of one Testament by the other.

It was this same passion for concatenation that prompted the medieval belief that as there were nine orders of angels, so were these distinguished by nine different jewels, and so were they duplicated in Hell by nine orders of devils and on earth by the nine orders of gentility namely Gentleman, Squire, Knight, Baron, Lord, Earl, Marquis, Duke, and Prince. Again, it was the same passion that connected the different ranks of human society with the different kinds of hunting hawks, allotting to a young man a hoby, to a lady a merlyn, to an Earl a peregrine, and so forth. And it was the same passion to connect that made medieval people cherish and develop their inheritance of the mystical significance of numbers and which, for instance, caused the chronicler Capgrave, when dedicating his chronicle to King Edward IV, to include the following sentences:

> I find a great convenience in your title, that ye be cleped Edward the Fourth. He that entered by intrusion was Harry the Fourth. He that entered by God's provision is Edward the Fourth. The similitude of the reparation is full like the work of the transgression, as the Church singeth in a preface: "Because Adam trespassed eating the fruit of a tree, therefore was Christ nailed on a tree."

A modern is likely to be faintly tickled or disgusted at a man's thus inflating the coincidence that the Lancastrian usurper of the Crown was the fourth of his name, while the legitimate Yorkist heir was fourth of his name also; and to think that it is indecorous or even blasphemous to bring the coincidence into so solemn a religious relation. Such thoughts would be far from troubling a medieval reader, who would have found Capgrave to have made an important point in a thoroughly recognised manner, to have promoted the understanding of the universe.

It is through bearing these matters in mind that we can understand why the Middle Ages fastened on certain parts of the apocryphal gospels and made much of them. Generally, these gospels took off from the canonical books of the New Testament. Often they merely embroidered; and in ways varying from the pleasantly picturesque to what strikes a modern reader as the purely frivolous. And such embroidery was legitimate by medieval standards. But sometimes a gospel was more serious, not embroidering but supplementing and fulfilling the text of Holy Writ. In so doing it was rendering a conspicuous service; for, just as medieval people believed that all wisdom was there in the stars if only you could extract it, so they believed that all religion was in Scripture if only you could see it, if only you could interpret in the right way what to fallible man appeared initially obscure, a mere hint perhaps but sufficient, if correctly taken, to divulge a wide area of truth. And always such a desire to interpret or supplement Scripture was part of the overriding desire to grasp and to concatenate all the phenomena of the universe as then known.

It now remains to explain how the myth of the Harrowing of Hell was pre-eminent in fulfilling the content of Scripture and in establishing connections with other events.

The idea of Christ rescuing Adam from Hell between his death and his resurrection came from a sublime imaginative effort to fulfil Scripture in its account of the central episode of the Christian creed and to establish connections within that episode. In the New Testament it is clearly asserted that through the fall of Adam he and all his progeny were incriminated: that a debt had been incurred that no ordinary man could fulfil, and that the Son of God chose out of his goodness to fulfil it through dying in human form; but nothing is said specifically about what happened to Adam when the debt was fulfilled. So, relying on vague texts to the effect that the spirit of Christ went and preached to the spirits in prison, interpreters of the Bible supplemented the text by defining what happened to Adam once the debt, what Milton called "the rigid satisfaction, death for death", was paid. The resultant myth was strictly logical. The moment Christ died, Adam could be freed; there was no need to wait for the Resurrection: and the central doctrine of the Redemption could be rounded off by Christ's rescuing Adam from Hell at the earliest possible moment. Was it not indeed self-evident that Christ would at once perform the act the performance of which was the very reason of his Incarnation and Passion? As to establishing connections, the concrete rescue of Adam by Christ corresponded precisely with the perdition of Adam by Satan through the concrete act of eating the forbidden fruit.

There is a special reason why the rescue of Adam, in itself so congenial to the imagination, should have been made prominent, indeed advertised, by medieval artists and writers. These men intended or were employed to *teach*; and what they produced was aimed largely at the eyes or the ears of illiterates, on whom they wished to make the deepest possible impression. To such recipients

Adam was Everyman, the embodiment of humanity, or, if you like, one of themselves. If the doctrine of the Redemption could be put in terms of Adam it would penetrate the simple man's mind more quickly and surely than through any other means. Looking at a mosaic or a fresco of Christ taking Adam by the hand, he could reflect: There am I; or there I could be, if I followed the commands of the Church.

Thus, the myth of the Harrowing of Hell and its reinforcement through art illustrate what I have already asserted: the strong practical effect of myth. Once a way of feeling or a mode of action has been embodied in the mythology of a large group of people it acquires an incalculable power. A healthy mythology is a nation's most precious possession.

John Speirs in his *Medieval English Poetry*, putting the question why the myth of the Harrowing of Hell spread so wide in the Middle Ages, gives the kind of anthropological answer he is apt to favour:

> *In the mythologies the descent of the hero or god into the underworld is one of the regular, if not essential episodes in his career. More specifically what we find enacted once again in the Play of the Harrowing of Hell, in a new form and with a new significance, is the age-old triumph of the sun-god over the demons of darkness.*

I am not convinced. When the medieval spectator saw the myth enacted in picture or on stage, he was in a different mood from one he might have been in at his own fireside of an evening. He was confronted with the attaining or the missing of his own salvation, and at that moment could spare no thought for the lore of Max

Müller. The myth of Adam's rescue from Hell in nearly every version belongs exclusively to medieval Christianity.

In the King's Chapel window, dating about 1530, the myth of the Harrowing of Hell appears in its full vigour. It suffered a decline, or rather an eclipse, very soon after. Through the action of the Council of Trent, the *Gospel of Nicodemus* was put on the Index for the years 1562-3; and artists ceased to show Christ haling Adam out of Limbo. I do not know why the Council of Trent acted thus; but at least it is obvious that apocryphal gospels, taken too seriously, would provide Scripture-intoxicated Protestants with excellent targets of attack, and it might be politic for Catholics to shuffle those targets conveniently away. One can only mourn the loss of one of the great achievements of the human imagination.

Anyone curious of finding out into what the great myth dwindled can satisfy his curiosity by consulting the commentaries on the Apostles' Creed. And I will add a word on what one of the most famous Protestant commentaries makes of the article in question.

In 1659 John Pearson published *An Exposition of the Creed*. It was immensely read and remained a theological classic well into the nineteenth century. Pearson was a remarkable man spanning the worlds before and after the English Civil War. He was born in 1613, studied at Queens' College, Cambridge, and contributed to the volume of elegies on Edward King, *Justa Edwardo King*, which contained Milton's *Lycidas*. His contribution, fourteen lines of Latin elegiacs, is competent but conventional. The gods, he says, protect Britain by the dangers of its seacoast. It is sad that the public safety should bring with it the loss by drowning of the glory of the Cantabrigian chorus. The conditions of such safety are too hard. A year after *An Exposition of the Creed*, Bishop Wren of Ely nominated Pearson Master of Jesus; and two years later he became Master of Trinity. More significantly he was elected Fellow of the Royal Society in 1667. He ended his career as Bishop of Exeter. Pearson was far more his true self as Fellow of the Royal Society than as contributor to a collection of pre-Civil War baroque elegies. His prose, which has not the least affinity with that of Browne or Jeremy Taylor and belongs solidly to the age of reason, is exquisitely lucid, a delight to read. Apart from the postulate that every word of Scripture is inviolate, Pearson conducts his inquiry with scrupulous regard to scientific truth. Does Scripture, he asks, truly corroborate the article of Christ's descent to Hell? He examines some of the texts usually thought to do so and dismisses them as inconclusive. Then, just as the foundations of ortho-doxy threaten to collapse, he finds in a passage in the Psalms and its interpretation in the Acts of the Apostles, along with Augustine's support, the evidence he needed. The article has been saved after all. And we can picture this Augustan divine wiping the sweat from his brow and going to his well-earned dinner.

Needless to say, Pearson has no use for the medieval notion that, attached to Hell, there was a Limbo, in which the virtuous Jews of before the Incarnation awaited their rescue by Christ:

> *I conclude that there is no certainty of truth in that proposition which the Schoolmen take for a matter of faith, that Christ delivered the souls of the saints from that place of Hell which*

*they call* limbus of the fathers, *into Heaven; and for that purpose after his death descended into Hell.*

No, according to Pearson, Christ descended into Hell to demonstrate by his return thence that it had no power over him and that he might experience the state of a dead man as well as that of a living one. And, in this second reason, he joins hands, surprisingly enough, with Langland. In a lovely passage where Langland states that you can conceive of joy only through experiencing sorrow, he adds that Christ went to Hell "to learn what all woe is". Thus Pearson was not quite removed from medieval sentiment. On the other hand, I know of no better way of estimating the distance between medieval and Augustan England than by first reading Langland's passus on the Harrowing of Hell and then the corresponding section of Pearson's *Exposition of the Creed.*

## 4. *The Harrowing of Hell in Medieval Literature*

Though there is an Anglo-Saxon version of the *Gospel of Nicodemus,* the theme of the Harrowing of Hell had to await the turn of the thirteenth and fourteenth centuries to become popular, to enter the hearts of the English people. Once this had happened, the literature of the late Middle Ages in England reposed on the authority and security of the great myth and was content to reproduce it unpretentiously and loyally. Only exceptionally did it add to the myth or seek to fashion it anew. On the other hand the literature is less uniform in treatment than is the art. For the artist the dramatic moment was when Christ, having burst the gates of Hell, took Adam by the hand;

and he always chose that moment however much else he succeeded in implying. In the literature the rescue of Adam is nearly always paramount, but sometimes with a different emphasis from the one dear to the artist.

Take an early fourteenth-century version, dramatic but not belonging to any of the great religious dramatic cycles. It is in the common rhymed octosyllabics, runs to 244 lines, and is easily accessible through being included in A. W. Pollard's *English Miracle Plays*.[1] Apart from a prologue and epilogue by the author, it consists of a monologue by Christ before the gates of Hell, a simple dialogue between Christ and Satan, Christ's call to the gate-keeper and his despairing cry, Christ's entry into Hell, where he is greeted first by Adam, then by Eve and others, and last the escape from Hell by the faithful. There is no repeated invocation of the gates, no taking of Adam by the hand. But it is entirely loyal to the myth, for the chief emphasis is firmly on Adam and his fate after the Crucifixion. Christ before Hell-gates says:

> *Adam, thou hauest dere aboht*
> *That thou levedest me noht;*
> *Adam, thou hauest aboht sore*
> *And I nil suffre that na more;*
> *I shal the bringe of helle pine*
> *And with me alle mine.*[1]

And, when Christ enters Hell, it is Adam who greets him

---

[1] Pages 166-72. Pollard reprints from the edition of Eduard Mall, *The Harrowing of Hell* (Breslau 1871).

[1] "Adam, you have paid a heavy price for not trusting me; Adam, you have paid a sharp price, and I will not allow this to continue. I will bring you out of the pains of Hell and all my own people along with me."

first. After Adam and Eve have spoken, Christ answers that he has given his life for them both. Finally the author in his epilogue applies the action of the piece to his fellow men:

> *Ah bring us out of helle pine,*
> *Louerd, ous and alle thine.*

The piece thus loyally corroborates the myth in its main object: the completion of the central doctrine of Christianity.

Or take the account of the Harrowing of Hell in the so-called Northern Passion, an early fourteenth-century poem in octosyllabics, perhaps from Durham. The author does no more than give a summary; and yet that summary has all the essentials, and especially the prominence of Adam. It is the rescue of Adam and Eve, balancing their primal sin, that is to the fore after Christ has made his supreme sacrifice. And the last lines imply the finality of Christ's redeeming act.

> *When Christ was ded thus als I tell,*
> *His godhede hastily went to hell,*
> *And sone he brak the yhates strang*
> *Ogayns him war thai sperd with wrang.*
> *The fendes war so sare adred*
> *If thai myght thai wild have fled,*
> *Bot ferrer may thai never fle,*
> *Thair herytage es thare to be.*
> *Sathanas he fested fast*
> *With bandes that sall euer last*
> *And so he sall be bonden ay*
> *Vn-till that it be domesday.*

*With him he toke Adam and Eve*
*And other that war to him leue:*
*Iohne the Baptist, Moyses al-swa,*
*Abraham and other ma,*
*That he had boght with payns fell,*
*All he led tham out of hell*
*And putt tham in-to Paradys,*
*Ware ioy as euer and endeles blys.*
*Thus that tre that gan us greue*
*Thurgh the first mysdede of Eue*
*Of the same our bote by-gan*
*Now when it bare both God and man.*[1]

But a mere summary is the exception. More often the authors love to dwell on the whole myth with all its details. Take, for example, *Cursor Mundi*, dating near the turn of the thirteenth and fourteenth centuries and written in the north of England, where there was a new translation of the *Gospel of Nicodemus* about this time. The poem, in the usual octosyllabics, might be more read if it were available in a more attractive form. Printed in four parallel versions in three enormous volumes of the Early English Text Society, it does anything but en-

[1] "And furthermore, when Christ was dead, his spirit went in haste to Hell. And soon he broke the strong gates that were wrongfully barred against him. The devils were so greatly afraid that they would have fled had they been able. But they may never flee beyond Hell, for it is their lot to stay there. He bound Satan fast with eternal bonds; and so shall Satan ever remain bound till the day of doom. He took with him Adam and Eve and others that were dear to him; John the Baptist, Moses too, Abraham and others, whom he had redeemed through his heavy pains—all these he led out of Hell and set in Paradise, where there is ever joy and endless bliss. Thus out of that very tree that made us suffer through Eve's primal sin began our salvation after it had carried him who was both God and man."

courage straightforward reading. In itself it reads pleasantly and it is remarkable in recounting in narrative what
the city guilds were about to present in dramatic form,
namely a series of sacred episodes extending from Creation
to Doomsday. The grand design of the medieval dramatic
cycles has had due recognition. For instance, A. P.
Rossiter wrote of the English cycles:

> *We may laugh at the* simplesse *which stages the Creation*
> (*as all four of our English cycles do*): *laugh outright at the*
> *account book's dry* "*Paid for the making of three worlds*
> *3d.*"; *but the magnificence of design of this Christian cosmic*
> *drama conterminous with Time's full extent is beyond denial.*

There is of course something very moving in the spectacle
of a group of men of varied capacities, some of them
doubtless very simple and reminiscent of Bottom's troupe
of actors, joining to turn the huge theme into living
drama; more moving than that of a single scholarly cleric
turning the same theme into rhymed octosyllabics. Yet
the author of *Cursor Mundi* deserves a portion of the
credit that goes to the dramatists for his courage in
attempting and completing his great venture. His treatment of the Harrowing of Hell, coming after he had
written over 17,000 lines, shows no relaxation of vitality.
He versifies the whole of the myth as found in the *Gospel
of Nicodemus* and adds touches of his own. For instance,
John the Baptist is not just there in Limbo along with the
rest but appears for the first time and joins them after the
light has shone in. Seth does not merely tell his story of
the oil of Paradise but is asked by Adam to tell it. Further,
the author seems to have taken the pictures of the myth
very much to heart, for he makes Christ take Adam by

the hand no less than three times. As in the King's windows, so in *Cursor Mundi* the Harrowing of Hell is made an episode of paramount importance.

All four complete play-cycles, York, Chester, Wakefield, and Coventry, include plays on the Harrowing of Hell, showing that in this department of medieval literature it was canonical.

Most orthodox and closest to the *Gospel of Nicodemus* and to *Cursor Mundi* is the Chester play. The stage directions are in Latin, and the author clearly knew the *Gospel of Nicodemus* at first hand. It is in a metre close to that of *Sir Thopas* and is well peppered with the kind of tag (*soth to say, iwis, withouten were*) that Chaucer ridicules through his parody. There is nothing distinguished about it either metrically or verbally. Yet, in spite of his shortcomings, in spite of our feelings that he is scarcely an autonomous literary entity, the author had a good sense of the stage. He disposes his material neatly, and the few things he adds to his original make for good drama. Supported by lively acting and a responsive audience, the play could have enjoyed high dramatic success. The author is loyal to the intention of the myth by making Adam prominent. Like the *Gospel of Nicodemus* in its Latin Version A the play opens with the shining of light into Hell and Adam's greeting of it. Other patriarchs speak, and Seth recounts his quest for the oil of mercy. Then there is a change of scene from Limbo to Hell with Satan sitting on his throne. Satan blusters at first and says that Christ on his arrival in Hell must be bound and kept there. But his underlings know the game is up and, when Christ commands the gates to open, tell Satan his power has gone and throw him from his throne. Christ, on entering Hell, takes Adam by the hand (*Tunc Iesus accipiet Adam per manum* is the stage direction), and says:

> Peace to the, *Adam, my darling,*
> *And eke to all thy ofspringe*
> *That righteous were in earth lyvinge;*
> *From me you shall not sever.*
> *To blisse now I will you bringe;*
> *Ther you shall be without endinge.*
> *Michael, lead these men singinge*
> *To joy that lasteth ever.*

And Michael does as he is bid. On their way to Heaven they are met by the three men who have never died, Enoch, Elijah, and the saved thief. This Chester play is the most conventional dramatic rendering in English of the myth of the Harrowing of Hell; it also corresponds the most closely to its representations in art.

The Coventry version is defective and consists of two separated fragments. The first fragment comes after Christ's death on the Cross and before the burial. Christ says he will go to Hell and rescue his friends. Arriving there he commands the gates to be raised, and Belial, despairing, gives in at once. Christ repeats that he will now fetch his friends; and the fragment ends abruptly. There is no irruption of light, and Adam is not mentioned. The second fragment is incorporated in the play of the Resurrection and shows Christ's soul returning to his body while the guards sleep, bringing with him Adam, Eve, Abraham, and others. He addresses Adam as if he were still in Hell and makes his present location even more inept by binding Belial. It is clear that the play does not survive in its original form.

The Wakefield *Harrowing of Hell* is one of the plays in this cycle derived from the York cycle and need not be considered separately.

To pass from any of the works I have touched on to the version of the myth in the York cycle is an exhilarating experience: for it is to pass from a little differentiated, communal drama, or from pleasant and competent mediocrity to a sophisticated, highly individual piece of artistry. On a smaller scale, it is like passing from minor Elizabethan drama to Shakespeare. The first thing one notices is the absence of those padding phrases that clog so much of medieval writing. These have been defended on rhetorical grounds: that they gave an audience points of rest and enabled it better to assimilate the remaining substance. But the true artist is loth to admit idle words; and the York dramatist, whose play contains only 400 lines, sees to it that all his words tell. Not only is he economical but he makes his words convey a number of different tones. For instance, Christ, prologising outside the gates of Hell, speaks in measured tones of pity and quiet benevolence:

> *Manne on molde, be meke to me*
> *And have thy Maker in thi mynde*
> *And thynke howe I have tholid for the*
> *With pereles paynes for to be pyned.*

But, commanding that Limbo should be opened up, he assumes the tones of a conqueror:

> *This steede schall stonde no lenger stoken;*
> *Opynne vppe and latte my pepul passe.*

After Christ's prologue, so mild in tone yet so indicative

of latent strength, the scene changes to Limbo, where Adam and the others use a speech much nearer to human conversation. And when the scene changes to Hell, the tone changes with it to an agitated chatter among the devils. And I could multiply instances of apt speech, if time allowed.

The structural skill equals the verbal, as in the following instances. Beginning and end, implication and extrication, are marked beautifully by words simultaneously in and out of the play; addressed equally to the players as players, and to them and the audience as real people.

> *Manne on molde, be meke to me*
> *And have thy Maker in thi mynde;*

those opening words are aimed equally at the audience and at the souls in Limbo. At the end, Michael, about to lead Adam and the rest to Heaven, asks Christ to bless them so that the devils may not molest them on their way. And in giving that blessing Christ includes audience as well as relevant actors, thus making the transition from imagined action to real life.

> *Mi blissing have ye all on rawe;*
> *I schall be with youe, wher ye wende;*
> *And all that lelly luffes my lawe*
> *Thai schall be blissid withowten ende.*[1]

And Adam, speaking the last quatrain of all, is at once Adam, Everyman, and all those present, actors and spectators together.

---

[1] "You have my blessing, all of you in order; where you go I shall be with you; and all who loyally love my law shall be blessed eternally."

*To the, Lorde, be louyng*
*That us has wonne fro waa;*
*For solas will we syng,*
Laus tibi cum gloria.[1]

It is right that Adam should speak the last word, for, as I have asserted, a main point of the play's original is that the story of the Redemption should be told as it affected Adam. But it is also right that Adam should be, in general time, Everyman and, even now, all the men present at the great dramatic festival. Next, the author knows how to yoke his scenes. The first three scenes represent Christ's prologue outside Hell, secondly the dialogue in Limbo, and last the dialogue in Hell; and the author brilliantly brings them together by making in the fourth scene Christ thunder without at the gates, Satan in Hell ask who is there, and David cry out the answer from Limbo. The climax is also brilliantly contrived. The action leads up to a great verbal duel between Christ and Satan, in which Satan comes to see that he does indeed confront the Son of God but gets great comfort from the assurance that Cain and other malefactors past and present will remain in his keeping. He breaks out in ungovernable glee, imagining his future successes, only to have his insolence crossed by Christ's telling Michael to bind him and by his ignominious fall into yet lower regions: a perfect reversal of situation in the manner recommended by Aristotle.

The devils, as often in the cycles, provide the occasion for comedy; and our author makes full use of it. He avoids

[1] "To thee, Lord, be praise, who hast won us from woe; for solace we will sing *Praise to thee with glory.*"

buffoonery and develops character. Discipline is not perfect in Hell. Satan (whose entry is carefully held back) is not very sure of himself and wants to get his underlings to do any unpleasant work. Beelzebub is a jealous second-in-command and not only insinuates doubts about his chief's power but taunts him as he sinks, bound, out of sight.

There is no time to specify the many delicate touches, whether of rhythm, or iteration, or implication that help to raise the play to a high aesthetic level. But I must add that the author remains entirely loyal to the engendering myth, while taking liberties with it. He omits Enoch, Elijah, and the saved thief, he inserts comedy in Hell. But the whole trend of the play is to corroborate the central aim of the myth, that of defining the part of Adam in the total action of the Redemption. He even adds definition by making Eve say, after Adam's initial greeting to the irrupting Christ, that they do not deserve to be rescued so soon, meriting more purgatory.

The other sophisticated and individual treatment of the Harrowing of Hell is Langland's. In some way he makes it the climax of his epic, but his treatment is so free and so peculiar that the myth almost loses its identity. Langland shows first-hand knowledge of the *Gospel of Nicodemus* and does in fact convey its intentions, but only through much mingling with other themes or in retrospect. His great and daring innovation was to combine another great medieval theme, that of the Four Daughters of God, with that of the Harrowing of Hell.

This new theme once more illustrates the medieval desire to extract a large meaning from a scriptural hint, the hint being the tenth verse of the eighty-fifth Psalm,

"Mercy and Truth are met together; Justice and Peace have kissed each other". It was agreed that this meeting and this osculation imply a previous conflict; but there were options as to the conflict's nature, for it could concern the rightness either of man's creation or of his redemption after his fall. Medieval preference was for the second application; and St Bernard's version of the myth was very briefly this. Man, as created, had four virtues: Pity, Truth, Justice, Peace. He lost them at the Fall; and in their separate, personified form, they became the Four Daughters of God. Pity and Peace remained man's advocates, while Truth and Justice insisted on making irrevocable the doom pronounced by God on man for his original sin. Pity and Peace pester God on man's behalf; and God summons the four to confer. To settle their dispute he invites Wisdom, in the form of Solomon, to pass judgement. Solomon says the doom is irrevocable without the atoning death of a sinless being. Truth and Pity search the earth and fail to find such a one. When Christ is sent to fill the gap, the Four Sisters meet and embrace.

Langland inserts this second myth into the Nicodeman narrative by picturing the Four Sisters coming from the four quarters of the earth to satisfy their curiosity about the unexpected light that shines onto Hell after Christ's death on the Cross. They have a long argument which Truth breaks off when she sees a spirit at the gates of Hell and hears him command them to be raised. And with Christ coming to claim his own and opposing Satan, the action of Hell's Harrowing is resumed. Christ binds Satan, and the passus proceeds to its ecstatic close with many hundreds of angels harping and singing and the

Four Daughters, now reconciled, dancing till the dawn of Easter morning.

In this free and new treatment of his theme, Langland not only relies on myth but adds to it and fashions it new. How far this re-fashioning was valid beyond himself, whether for his audience it became a classic and operative version of the myth, alternative to the more conventional versions, cannot be told; but at least we can assert that it possesses the quality to do so.

I said earlier that the story of Christ's descent into Hell showed in almost all versions no kinship with pagan folklore. And I made the qualification because in a single passage Langland may show himself the exception. Before treating of the descent, Langland speaks of the darkness over the earth and the earthquake that followed Christ's death. Then, in describing how the graves open and a dead man prophesies, he seems for a moment to get out of the purely Christian content into a more general world of primitive legend and belief:

> Ded men for that dyne come out of depe graues
> And told whi that tempest so longe tyme dured.
> "For a bitter bataille", the ded bodye sayde,
> "Lyf and deth in this darknesse; her one fordoth her other.
> Shal no wighte wite witterly who shal have the maystrye
> Er sondey aboute sonne rysynge". And sank with that til
> erthe.[1]

On this point there is no evidence for argument, and one

---

[1] "Because of that noise, dead men came out of deep graves and told why that storm lasted so long. 'Because of a bitter fight,' the dead body said, 'life and death in this darkness—one destroys the other. No man shall know for certain who shall prevail till Sunday about dawn.' And the body sank into earth."

is at the disposal of one's impressions. And all I can do is to record my impression that here the Christian doctrine of Christ's struggle with death merges into universal myths of light fighting darkness and of life fighting death. If my impression is true, it reinforces my plea that Langland's treatment of our myth is uniquely individual and comprehensive.

To end this section and to make it more emphatic I will ask you to recall the Chinese poem, *On the Frontier*, which I read last time, and to compare it with the poems having the Harrowing of Hell as their subject. The first can be fully grasped and appreciated by one person reading it in isolation; any sharing of the experience it offers consists in the power of all normal men individually to appreciate the poem as he does. But the poems that derive from the Gospel of Nicodemus depend on an agreement within a large group of men that here is something significant, something that should direct their ways of thinking and doing. And if the individual of today is to understand and enjoy the York play, for instance, he must identify himself imaginatively with the people for whom the play's subject has this special significance.

## III. TWO TUDOR MYTHS

### 1. Preface

THE Elizabethans took history in a much less detached way than we do, objectivity being for them no virtue; and as they saw in nature allegorical pictures of human states of mind, so they associated past happenings with their own moral and political problems. In the deeds of the great men of the past they saw examples of what the great men of today should emulate or avoid; from the way past events revealed the workings of general principles of cause and effect they hoped to derive practical guidance in the conduct of state affairs. Of course the Elizabethans enjoyed the *Lives* of Plutarch for their entertainment value but they also took them most seriously as the best repertory of exemplary deeds that existed. The falls of great men recounted in grim monotony in *A Mirror for Magistrates* not only satisfied that craving for melancholy that besets simple people when personally they are in exceptionally good spirits, but was thought to have a practical bearing on modern political conduct. If a contemporary prince, it was thought, read and took to heart the lessons that emerged so obviously from the stories in the *Mirror*, he was more likely to avoid errors and to make the right decisions. Further, there were definite lessons that could be learnt from the way past history evolved. For instance, it was thought that in a royal line a thing that happened in one generation was likely to repeat itself in the third. Such knowledge was allowed

45

to have practical value. Thinking thus, the Elizabethans would be more prone than most other generations of men to isolate and make important certain political events and ideas, in other words to make myths of them.

The two political myths that are the subject of this section derived from two very different places: the first from the shakiness of Henry VII's title to the English throne; the second from the horror of civil war planted in men's minds by the Wars of the Roses.

## 2. *The Myth of Pedigree*

Owen Tudor, grandfather of Henry VII, came of a good but un-ennobled Welsh family. Through his mother he was related to Owen Glendower, famous as figuring in Shakespeare's *Henry IV*; and it is probable that Tudor got his footing in the court of Henry V through the influence of Glendower's son, who had employment there. Tudor may or may not have been one of the Welsh band that distinguished itself at Agincourt, but he stayed in Henry's train till his death. Then he became Clerk of the Wardrobe to Henry's widow, Catherine de Valois, Shakespeare's Kate in *Henry V*. Nothing is known of how he captured the Queen Dowager's affections, and our imaginations have free play in the matter. I like to think of this Welsh adventurer, gifted with the oratory of his race, working on the sense of exile they both felt among the slower-witted English, until each found the other's company indispensable. It is uncertain whether there was an actual marriage, but Catherine bore him three sons and two daughters, who, whether born in or out of wedlock, were later made or re-made legitimate by Parliament. While Henry VI was a minor, the state of his half-brothers was precarious; but when he came of age he advanced his kin and made the eldest, Edmund, Earl of Richmond. He also arranged a match between him and the Lancastrian noblewoman, Lady Margaret Beaufort. These two were the parents of Henry VII. Unfortunately the suspicion of illegitimacy was not confined to Henry's paternal side, for Lady Margaret's Lancastrian ancestry was from the third consort of John of Gaunt, Catherine Swinford, whose children by him, born out of wedlock, owed their later legitimacy to the action of Parliament. Further, even if Lady Margaret were recognised as the genuine Lancastrian heiress, there was still Elizabeth of York, daughter of Edward IV, whom Henry did indeed marry after becoming king but who could always be considered as a woman deprived of her due status of reigning monarch.

Thus, conspicuously weak in his ancestral credentials, no wonder if Henry set about strengthening them by the creation of myths. We do not know whether this was his own idea, but it would be in keeping with his character if this were so. Possibly the thing entered his head when he perceived the enthusiasm with which the Welsh greeted him as a distinguished scion of their race when he landed at Milford Haven to claim the crown. Before mentioning the forms of Henry's mythical inventions I must remind you of the different ways of feeling now and in the Tudor epoch about the component races of England. We are taught that we are primarily Anglo-Saxons and that the germs of our political institutions and privileges are to be found in Saxon times. Such notions were foreign to the generality of men in the Tudor epoch, who did not feel more warmly about Saxons than about Britons or Normans. Further, they were much better instructed in the fabulous history of the Britons than we are, through the vogue of Geoffrey of Monmouth's history of the kings of Britain, compiled in the twelfth century, narrating the Trojan ancestry of the British kings through Brutus, great-grandson of Aeneas, the acts of the pre-Christian British kings including those of Lear, and the glories of Arthur and his knights in the centuries after Christ. A minority of more critical folk had always questioned the truth of these fables, but in general Englishmen as well as Welshmen liked them and found them instructive; and in particular they thought they had as good a stake in Arthur as anyone else. And Arthur was worth having a stake in for he was one of the Nine Worthies of the medieval world; and did not Mrs Quickly asseverate of the dead Falstaff, "Nay, sure, he's not in Hell: he's in Arthur's bosom, if ever man went to Arthur's bosom"? It was through this vogue of the lore of Albion that Henry was able to impose his first myth on England.

This myth had two parts. The first was connected with King Arthur. A detail of the Arthur legend was that, like Barbarossa and Lord Kitchener, he did not die but that he would reappear in the fullness of time. Henry VII fostered the notion that in some way the House of Tudor realised this detail of the legend. He did not claim to be Arthur reincarnate himself but he wanted his house to re-enact the glory Britain enjoyed in Arthurian days; and that was why his eldest son was christened Arthur. Secondly, Henry had his personal legend. Cadwallader, called the blessed, was a historical character, a Welshman who came to live in England and died about the year 664. Geoffrey of Monmouth made much more of him. He fabled that his father Cadwalla, of the royal house of Wales, inheriting from his father all England south of the Humber, killed Edwin, King of the Northumbrians and finally subdued the whole of England, which he ruled for forty-eight years. His son Cadwallader succeeded him and was the last king of the united island. Henry VII claimed descent from Cadwallader. How seriously he did so can be seen from the life of Henry, written by Bernardus Andreas sometimes known as André of Toulouse. André was attached to Henry during Henry's exile in Brittany and France, may have landed with him at Milford Haven, and was certainly present at Henry's triumphal entry into London. Henry made him his Poet Laureate and tutor to his eldest son, Arthur, and André in his history calls himself Historiographer Royal. It is certain that what André said was what Henry wished him to say; and one of his acts was to magnify his master's ancestry. He did his job thoroughly, proclaiming generally that by the antiquity and nobility of his descent Henry VII excelled all Christian princes past and present. Chief among his claims to distinction was descent from Cadwallader and through him from Brutus himself, founder of the British race.

Fantastic as Henry's claims were, they had their effect and they persisted not merely through the whole house of Tudor but into the house of Stuart right up to the Civil War.

This, the first of the Tudor myths, inspired only one piece of great literature, Spenser's *Fairy Queen*. The topic is complicated and has had full treatment, conspicuously in Greenlaw's classic *Studies in Spenser's Historical Allegory*. It would, if pursued, occupy a disproportionate part of these lectures; and I therefore omit it. Instead, I will illustrate the myth's vogue in two less important places.

William Warner's *Albion's England*, a narrative poem epitomising history from Noah to Queen Elizabeth, however little suited to modern taste, was greatly liked in its own day. It follows Golding's Ovid in being in four-teeners and maintained its popularity from 1586, when it was published, till at least 1602, when it enjoyed its final enlargement. Meres in 1598 cited the poem as an example of English epic capable of matching foreign masterpieces, adding that he had heard the best wits of both our universities term Warner our English Homer. *Albion's England* is one of those works that retain little literary interest but possess great sociological interest as showing what was central and typical of its age. When it makes much of the first Tudor myth, we may be certain that the Elizabethans generally made much of it too. Warner introduces it through his account of how the widowed Queen Catherine conveyed her passion for her comparatively humble Clerk of the Wardrobe. Owen Tudor is quick to see the position and to reassure the queen that their differences in rank are not what she supposes, although it may be true that he cannot compare in worldly goods.

> But (for I will disperse the mists of further mysteries
> And tug the pinnace of my thoughts to keening of your eyes)
> If gentry, madam, might convey so great a good to me,
> From ancient King Cadwallader I have my pedigree.

*If wealth be said my want, I say your Grace doth want no wealth,*
*And my supplyment shall be love, employed to your health.*

Indeed, Warner shows Owen well able to profit by his good fortune. And later, commenting on the Battle of Bosworth, Warner proclaims that the descendants of Aeneas can now no more "of orphansy complain", thus joining Henry VII, as André of Toulouse had done, with the fabulous genealogies of Geoffrey of Monmouth.

Not less popular than *Albion's England* were Drayton's *England's Heroical Epistles*, first published in 1597 and imitating Ovid's *Heroides*. They are in the heroic couplet and are much more readable than Warner. Of these letters one is from Queen Catherine to Owen Tudor; and the next is his answer. In her letter Catherine has quite grasped the eminence of Owen's pedigree and even enlarges on reasons why her great kin (her father, her husband, her brother were all kings) cannot object to their marriage as being unequal. Children of King John and Edward I had been given in marriage to the royal Llewelyns of Wales,

> *Showing the greatness of your blood thereby,*
> *Your race and royal consanguinity.*
> *And Wales, as well as haughty England, boasts*
> *Of Camelot and all her Pentecosts;*
> *To have precedence in Pendragon's race*
> *At Arthur's table challenging the place.*

Owen in his answer is equally emphatic:

> *By our great Merlin was it not foretold*
> *(Amongst his holy prophecies enrolled),*

51

*When first he did of Tudor's name divine,*
*That kings and queens should follow in our line,*
*And that the helm (the Tudor's ancient crest)*
*Should with the golden flower-de-luce be dressed;*
*As that the leek (our country's chief renown)*
*Should grow with roses in the English crown?*

And there is much more about the Tudor pedigree and the glory of Wales in repelling invaders and keeping their speech in spite of Saxon, Danish, and Norman intrusion.

It is hard for us to credit that so crudely trumped up a business as the Tudors descent from fabulous British kings could achieve mythical force. We can believe that it could attain to being an academic game for the few, but that it could be the theme of serious talk in homes and taverns, that it should live in the mouths of men, seems impossible. One reason for supposing that it did live indeed is its figuring in the pageantry that was so important in the popular entertainment of the time; in the shows that accompanied coronations, weddings, births, and the progresses of royalty. That we cannot know precisely the vitality of the myth is certain, but it is equally certain that this vitality exceeded anything that by modern standards we can find credible. What, for instance are we to make of the following fact? Dr John Dee, Welshman, Fellow of Trinity, renowned mathematician and cosmographer, and intimate of the Queen, maintained that Greenland and Estotiland and perhaps Newfoundland had been colonised by King Arthur and hence were British possessions.[1] There indeed is myth given a practical application.

[1] I owe this reference to A. L. Rowse, *The Elizabethans and America* (London 1959), 17-19.

### 3. The Myth of Divine Appointment

Whatever the degree of vitality of the first Tudor myth, we have no difficulty in recognising the power of the second: that based on memories of the Wars of the Roses and on the hope that these would not be repeated. When the Tudors created or allowed to be created a myth of history embodying these memories and this hope, they did something we can understand and the success of which seems to us to have a strong initial chance of survival. The myth, which in general terms was that the Tudors had been divinely appointed to put an end to a long spell of civil war and to lead the country out of an unspeakable tyranny into happiness, had to wait for its full elaboration till the time of Henry VIII; but from André of Toulouse it is clear that Henry VII set it going. André recounts the speeches that the Earl of Richmond and Richard III made before the Battle of Bosworth (speeches which may be imaginary but which must be the ultimate source of the speeches in Shakespeare's *Richard III*); and he makes Richmond say "Non ferro, non igne, non praeda te [*sc.* patriam] populare volumus sed a tyrannide liberare" ("We do not intend to devastate the country by the sword or fire or rapine but to free it from tyranny"), while Richard calls for indiscriminate slaughter: in particular let Richmond be killed without pity or, better still, let him be captured so that he may be put to unheard-of tortures. There indeed we have the myth in embryo.

The practical value of this second myth in strengthening the Tudors and of any writings that succeeded in supporting it is too obvious to need comment.

Of the various versions of English history in its evolution from the troubled days of Richard II, through the glorious interlude of Henry V and the miseries of the Wars of the Roses to the peace of the Tudors, that of Hall in the reign of Henry VIII is the most complete and philosophical; it is also the version used by Shakespeare. I have given a summary of it in my book on Shakespeare's History Plays and do not wish to give it again. It is also more apt now to indicate some version of the second Tudor myth simpler than that of Hall; which was current only among the more sophisticated members of the community, the generality not being concerned with Hall's elaborate schemes of cause and effect. A better place to find the popular version is, for instance, Warner's *An Epitome of the whole History of England*, printed as an appendix to the 1602 edition of *Albion's England*. These are the main points of this version. The English civil wars were not confined to the Wars of the Roses but began in the reign of Richard II and extended right through the reign of Henry VII till finally extinguished with the reign of Henry VIII. Richard II asked for trouble; yet his deposition was a crime, and civil war continued in the reign of his successor. The reign of Henry V was a glorious interlude in evil times. The fullest rigour of civil war began in the reign of Henry VI, after the Dukes of Gloucester and Bedford died. Although civil war continued in the form of several unsuccessful insurrections in the age of Henry VII, the turning-point came in the reign of his predecessor, Richard III. It was during his reign that the workings of Providence were most evident. Richard was an unparalleled villain, *a most faithless usurper and blood-insatiate tyrant, of whom to be delivered, to Godwards or the Devil, were wanting neither prayers nor curses. This God-left man, having by exquisite hypocrisy, numerous and execrable murders, opened unto himself way to the kingdom, reigned with like-continued tyranny. Insomuch that of the nobility many fled the land, most the court, and all studied better times and their own safeties.*

Although it was not given to Henry VII to bring civil war quite to an end, he was the principal agent of God in the process. Of Richard III and his end at Bosworth Warner wrote:

*Wherein is to be observed the unscrutable providence of the Almighty, who, when it so pleaseth him, even from most bad causes produceth most good effects. For had not this tyrant (though far off from conceiting any such happy event to the weal-public) made riddance of so many of the then factious families that might, and no doubt in their turns would, have been competitors of the sovereignty, wherethrough aptly survived an indubitate heir male of the one house and an indubitate heir female of the other, either of them marriageable and neither of them married; and had he not reigned so odiously that the two factious houses, sundering in all things else, of necessity concurred to suppress him their common enemy; the so bloody and long-continued civil wars had still lived an Hydra, whereunto the then studied union by this opportune marriage, plotted and afterwards effected, was thenceforth (and for ever may it be so) an Hercules.*

To interpret Warner's simile strictly, it was not the mere marriage of Henry VII to Elizabeth of York that was the

Hercules but the fruit of it as well. It was reserved to Henry VIII to be quite accepted as the lawful sovereign and to fulfil God's purposes in another most conspicuous way, namely through freeing England from papal tyranny. Elizabeth continued the great Tudor tradition by keeping the land free from this tyranny and from the civil war of which papal intrigue was the most dangerous instrument.

In this or some other simplified form the second Tudor myth was the possession of almost the whole population of England. Thus diffused, it was both a powerful political force and the potential material of popular literature; and the man who best seized that potentiality was Shakespeare.

Through the date of his birth, 1564, Shakespeare was peculiarly exposed to the impact of the Tudor myth, for it was in his formative years that the truth of the myth was subject to its severest trials. In 1568 Mary Queen of Scots, thought by Catholic extremists to be the lawful heir of the English throne, took refuge with Elizabeth; which happening was the signal of repeated insurrections or intrigues against the existing settlement. In 1569 and 1570 there were risings in the north, fomented by the Catholic nobility of that part of England; and at the age of five and six Shakespeare may well have seen levies passing through Stratford for their suppression. These rebellions provoked a new Church Homily, *Against Disobedience and wilful Rebellion*, for reading in all churches. In the same year as the second rebellion the Pope excommunicated Queen Elizabeth, and thenceforward her assassination could count as an act of piety among the faithful. In 1572, when Shakespeare was eight, the greatest nobleman of the land, the Duke of Norfolk, was executed for sharing in a Catholic plot to depose Elizabeth and instate Mary. The same year saw the Massacre of St Bartholemew in Paris. And the period of trial continued till the execution of Mary and the Spanish Armada shortly after. Thus it was that Shakespeare's formative years coincided with a period when the Tudor myth took on a new vitality just because it was threatened, the very threat serving only to ratify and to corroborate it.

It cannot be proved, but it is morally certain, that in these formative years Shakespeare supplemented the knowledge of the Tudor myth he must have acquired from the talk of those he grew up with and from the doctrine he heard in church, by his reading of Hall's *Chronicle*, the political doctrines of which permeate his history plays and are especially prominent in his earlier historical tetralogy, the three parts of *Henry VI* and *Richard III*. And it is in these plays that we can see as good an example as it is possible to find of works owing their origin, and much of their power, to a myth cherished by almost the whole community. That this should be so is the reverse of surprising. A genius, however original, needs the support of conventions or of public themes in his early efforts. As his stature grows, he will need that support less; and when it is complete, he will create myths rather than use existing ones. Shakespeare demonstrates the process to perfection.

Rich in promise but still immature and developing, Shakespeare needed the support of a current myth and the great popular backing it had, to achieve the grand conceptions and the nobility of shaping that give the

Henry VI plays their quality. In spite of obvious weaknesses these declare a sense of confidence, of the man's knowing he is doing the right kind of thing, that makes those weaknesses strangely innocuous. And then in *Richard III* Shakespeare achieves, certain faults apart, the perfection of this kind of writing.

I will omit the Henry VI plays and confine myself to *Richard III* for illustration of my thesis. In spite of many individual touches his Richard is still the orthodox monster of the myth, those touches serving to animate him, not to detach him from it. And for all his prominence he is not the centre of the play, which remains, as it had been in the three earlier plays, the native land and her fate. Nor is there the least sense that Shakespeare wanted it to be otherwise. For all his proclivities to make living people, he is now content that sharpness of character should yield to the impersonal workings of God's will, that realism should yield to ritual, and that the author's idiosyncrasies should be swallowed up in the public sentiments which he is content to reverence. These assertions are especially true of the last parts of the play. These parts are strictly loyal to the details of the myth. One of these details, the union created by the monstrosities of Richard among the former enemies, you will remember was made much of by Warner. Shakespeare, through his use of it, achieves the peculiar perfection of which I have spoken. In a passage that owes nothing to the chronicles he makes Richard's very mother join the other side and curse her son. Her final speech is true Shakespeare and yet in the unobtrusiveness of its intensity it shows utter and willing subordination to the public theme it pronounces:

*Either thou wilt die by God's just ordinance*
*Ere from this war thou turn a conqueror;*
*Or I with grief and extreme age shall perish*
*And never more behold thy face again.*
*Therefore take with me my most grievous curse,*
*Which in the day of battle tire thee more*
*Than all the complete armour that thou wearest!*
*My prayers on the adverse party fight;*
*And there the little souls of Edward's children*
*Whisper the spirits of thine enemies*
*And promise them success and victory.*
*Bloody thou art, bloody will be thy end;*
*Shame serves thy life and doth thy death attend.*

Shakespeare expands this theme of the Yorkists forsaking
Richard in the episode of Richard's being visited in his
sleep before the Battle of Bosworth by the ghosts of the
people, Lancastrians and Yorkists, whom he has killed.
In the chronicles the apparitions were not of murdered
men but "divers images like terrible divels, which pulled
and haled him, not suffering him to take any quiet and
rest". Shakespeare converts these vague tormentors into
the ghosts of characters whom we know well already
from the Henry VI plays and makes them conduct a
solemn ritual of commination and benediction addressed
not to Richard only but to both sleeping leaders. In the
ritual there are of course many repetitions; but by his
delicate variations Shakespeare raises the scene to great
beauty. The ghost of Henry VI addresses the rivals
thus:

*When I was mortal, my anointed body*
*By thee was punched full of deadly holes.*

*Think on the Tower and me; despair and die!*
*Harry the Sixth bids thee despair and die.*

*Virtuous and holy, be thou conqueror!*
*Harry, that prophesied thou shouldst be king,*
*Doth comfort thee in thy sleep: live and flourish!*

Then the ghost of Clarence follows:

*Let me sit heavy in thy soul tomorrow,*
*I, that was washed to death with fulsome wine,*
*Poor Clarence, by thy guile betrayed to death.*
*Tomorrow in the battle think on me*
*And fall thy edgeless sword. Despair and die!*

*Thou offspring of the house of Lancaster,*
*The wronged heirs of York do pray for thee.*
*Good angels guard thy battle! Live and flourish!*

As in the Duchess of York's speech, the beauty Shakespeare reaches here does not contaminate his task as the mouthpiece of strong public feelings; again he is willingly loyal to the great myth. And he finally ratifies his loyalty in the last lines of the play, when Richmond, a quite flat character, in conventional and yet most moving words both sums up the course of past events and gives the Tudor myth an immediate, contemporary application. Like the author of the York Harrowing of Hell play, Shakespeare in his last lines of all is both in and out of his play, making Richmond speak to fellow-characters and audience at the same time.

*England hath long been mad and scarred herself:*
*The brother blindly shed the brother's blood;*

*The father rashly slaughtered his own son;*
*The son, compelled, been butcher to the sire;*
*All this divided York and Lancaster,*
*Divided in their dire division,*
*O now let Richmond and Elizabeth,*
*The true succeeders of each royal house,*
*By God's fair ordinance conjoin together!*
*And let their heirs, God, if thy will be so,*
*Enrich the time to come with smooth-faced peace,*
*With smiling plenty and fair prosperous days.*
*Abate the edge of traitors, gracious Lord,*
*That would reduce the bloody days again*
*And make poor England weep in streams of blood.*
*Let them not live to taste the land's increase,*
*That would with treason wound this fair land's peace.*
*Now civil wounds are stopped, peace lives again:*
*That she may live long here, God say amen!*

Having reached a certain kind of perfection, Shakespeare could not repeat it. He had reached an ultimate, from which he could only turn back. It may well be that it was this predicament that caused him to abandon any plans he had made for continuing the Tudor myth by writing, as Hall had done, on the glorious age of Henry VIII. Be that as it may, when he turned to history once more, the time was passed when he could give himself to the myth so thoroughly. In *Richard II* and *Henry IV* he claims a new breadth for his expanding genius; and the myth must perforce coexist with other things. This he could do without disloyalty, for the myth itself was not very exacting in its details during this stretch of history. He was not offending against it when he enlarged a

61

slender tradition into the massive creations of Falstaff and
his fellows. It was only in his next play that there was a
conflict. The myth of Henry V as the perfect king, beloved of the people, was a kind of autonomous submyth
in the larger complex: anyhow too powerful to be disregarded or altered. It may be that Shakespeare's reluctance or even resentment in having to submit to this
necessary restriction accounts for the defects of his play.

The process Shakespeare had gone through was not
only that of discarding the need to rely on a myth; it was
also that of learning to make myths. Already through
Shylock he had added to the stock of his country's
mythology. Another addition, Falstaff, was not only an
addition but the means of a new freedom. Once Falstaff
had captured the hearts of the playgoers, Shakespeare
could make them take from him pretty much what he
wanted: even something as austere as *Coriolanus*. Some
years ago Cambridge supplied an example of a similar
state of affairs between author and audience. The Arts
Theatre had the temerity to put on Eliot's *Family Reunion*
during a particularly dead time of the Long Vacation,
when no undergraduates were in residence. I went and
found the theatre full, but with an audience I should have
thought unlikely to have much use for the play: some, for
instance, were employees of a local factory, sent to listen
by a kindly management. The audience took the play
not merely with respect but with a fascinated interest.
"Here," you could guess them saying to themselves, "is
big stuff. I couldn't tell you what it's all about but I'm
getting something from it and I'm glad I have come."
And then it occurred to me that the reason why they
were letting the play work thus upon them was that it

was by the author of *Murder in the Cathedral*, Eliot's one play that has definitely captured the *popular* imagination. To revert to Shakespeare, I do not mean that he disregarded the conventions of his art; within these he was always ready to work: but this is quite different from accepting the help of a myth. *Hamlet* remains an Elizabethan revenge-play while making Shakespeare's biggest contribution to our national mythology.

What strikes me so forcibly in this development of Shakespeare is its rightness. He got the very best out of the chances that came his way. He was not too proud to accept help when he needed it; he was too independent a spirit to go on accepting that help when he was past needing it. He was the supreme opportunist; and quite exempt from the dishonesty that opportunism is likely to bring with it. In the matter of myth he is the perfect model of how to use it and then, having done so, how to create it.

Having spoken in general of what the myth meant to Shakespeare and how he used it, let me end with a single detail. There is every reason to think that he accepted the total myth both in its rudimentary form and as elaborated by Hall. As I have just described, the reign of Henry VIII was an organic part of it. Why then did Shakespeare not go on from Richard III to include this reign? And why, not having done so, did he pick up the theme at the very end of his dramatic career? These are questions not usually put, the play of *Henry VIII* itself supplying puzzles enough to satisfy normal curiosity. The first puzzle is of course authorship. Till recently it was orthodox to accept the double authorship of Shakespeare and Fletcher; now opinion has turned towards trusting the First Folio and its editors and believing that they knew what they were doing in their decisions on what to include. *Henry VIII* is in the First Folio; and its latest editor, R. A. Foakes, gives Shakespeare credit for the whole play. I do not want to enter the controversy, but at least I believe that Shakespeare was responsible for the play's initiation, and generally for its contents, whether or not he wrote every scene and every word. If this position is allowed, I can go on to a smaller but significant puzzle, which I do not remember having seen referred to, the prologue. Why should the prologue be so inadequate an account of what is to follow? It warns the hearer of the extreme pathos of the contents, things

> *That bear a weighty and a serious brow,*
> *Sad, high, and working, full of state and woe;*
> *Such noble scenes as draw the eye to flow.*

It goes on to disclaim any merriment or bawdry and it ends by repeating what it had made foolproof-clear at the beginning: that the play is dismal, depicting great men in high prosperity;

> *then, in a moment see*
> *How soon this mightiness meets misery:*
> *And, if you can be merry, then I'll say*
> *A man may weep upon his wedding day.*

On a balance it is doubtful if the play is dismal; it is not a mere mirror for magistrates, though partly akin to that mode. Nor is the disclaimer of mirth and bawdry correct, witness among other places Act 2, Scene 3, between Anne Bullen and the Old Lady. As the play proceeds it emerges from calamity into prosperity. Cranmer escapes his judges;

there is the pomp of a happy coronation; Anne Bullen and Cromwell are presented at the height of their fortunes; and the play ends with the triumphal prophecy of the golden ages to come. Even the falls of the great are softened by the humility with which these accept the changes of fortune; they have forsaken the cruder melodrama of the 'mirror' tradition. One could heap up conjecture why prologue should not match text. It might be that the prologue was meant for a different, earlier, play on the falls of the great in the age of Henry VIII. Be that as it may, the parts of the play the prologue fails to cover complete those items in the Tudor historical myth which Shakespeare had not included in his play-cycle from *Richard II* to *Richard III*. Henry stands out as the unchallenged king of England and, though impetuous and not quite sure in his judgement, emerges as on the whole good. There is a strong Protestant tone; and the Reformation is presented as a blessing. And there is the glorification of Elizabeth and her golden age through the glowing picture given of her mother and through Cranmer's great speech near the end. Although there is not the least sign that Shakespeare's style in the play is anything but late, it is difficult to resist the thought that the scenes of triumph and prosperity represent the fulfilment of something he had meant to do many years before. Though there may have been topical reasons for Shakespeare's turning once more to political drama, I do not believe that at so late a period of his life he would have submitted to doing so, had not the seeds of what he came to write been lying dormant in his brain; dormant, but, when refreshed, irritating and provocative until allowed to sprout and bear fruit.

# IV. AGGRESSION

THE contrary human impulses indicated in such twin phrases as aggression and withdrawal, action and contemplation, adventure and consolidation, are so fundamental and permeating that one would not expect them to provide myths any more than we expect eating and sleeping to do so. It can happen, however, that at some point in history one opposing partner much preponderates over the other, makes men aware of that preponderance and ends by creating a myth of that awareness. One way of keeping a balance between the partners was to allot each to a different order of society. It was the medieval way, where the proneness of the knightly class to action was balanced by the proneness of the monastic class to contemplation. With the sixteenth century in western Europe there entered a general awakening of man's active side, while in England the suppression of the monasteries deprived men of their main outlet on the contemplative side. Such a deprivation was felt less while the general urge in the other direction was strong. In the Elizabethan age, what with new lands to explore, a new religious settlement to consolidate, and a constantly threatening enemy to ward off, we do not feel any impoverishment of the human spirit because the opportunities for contemplation were curtailed.

Along with the general awakening of man's active side in the sixteenth century went the urge to exceptional individual prowess. Indeed there was the sheer need for it, if the nations of western Europe were to exploit the possibilities offered to them in the new world. And, in view of that need, no wonder if the cult of the superior man became one of the myths of the age. There were two kinds of superior man: the all-round kind and the excessive kind. One was the Governor or Courtier; and he, though first a man of action, was also versed in theory, a Platonist, anyhow not so utterly given to the active life as to have lost a proper human poise. His myth received many embodiments, one of the most eminent and typical in English being in Sidney's *Arcadia,* where Pyrocles and Musidorus, Pamela and Philoclea, are all superlative in their courage or beauty or courtly bearing or political sagacity. We can verify the genuineness of the myth by reflecting how impossible it would be to accept these creations of Sidney in contexts of a hundred or two hundred years later. The excessive kind was usually bad, or at least his excesses were usually to be deplored or pitied, but he could be, by Elizabethan standards, good. An example is Shakespeare's Talbot in *Henry VI, Part I,* whose excessive ferocity is equated with his love of king and country, of which there cannot be too much. But whether the excessive man were good or bad, his myth existed just because for the Elizabethans uncommon deeds by uncommon men had a very special fascination. But though, thus fascinated, the Elizabethans were prone to judge the excessive man kindly, there were limits to that kindness; and there was bound to be a conflict between an excessive man who had passed those limits, and a society initially favourable to him but convinced that those limits must be respected. Naturally it was the dramatists who made chief use of this conflict; and

Marlowe's Faustus and Jew, Shakespeare's Aaron, Chapman's Bussy, and Jonson's Volpone are conspicuous characters illustrating it. The myth of the superior man quickly lost its power as the seventeenth century proceeded; but there is an interesting survival in one of the later dramatists of the great tradition, Ford. The nominal theme of his *'Tis Pity She's a Whore* is incest, but its basic theme is that of two superior persons, in potential merit far exceeding all other characters in the play, driven by a cruel fate to monstrous acts and inevitably brought to ruin. Giovanni's words as he is about to kill his Arrabella both define the true subject of the play and hint at the myth it embodies.

> *If ever after-times should hear*
> *Of our fast-knit affections, though perhaps*
> *The laws of conscience and of civil use*
> *May justly blame us, yet when they but know*
> *Our loves, that love will wipe away that rigour*
> *Which would in other incests be abhorred.*

In other words, really superior characters deserve special treatment. No other play of Ford has the energy of *'Tis Pity*; and it owes this uniqueness to the power of the myth behind it. In contradiction the excessive characters of the Heroic Play of the Restoration, deriving not from a true myth but from a frigid doctrine of decorum, fail to be convincing.

The seventeenth century did indeed see a reaction from the aggressive spirit of the former century and a movement towards the balancing spirit of withdrawal; witness, for a single example, the religious community of Little Gidding. Nevertheless, the aggressive spirit per-

sisted in a single quarter. It is now a commonplace that
the most rigid form of Protestantism was in accord with
the age in which it arose, and that Calvin's Elect represent
in their way the contemporary exaltation of the superior
man. (Holy Willie, Burns's Calvinist Elder, argues with
God very much in the sense of Giovanni's words over
Arrabella.) The religion of English puritanism, deriving
largely from Calvin, in its early vigour ("plain, simple,
sullen, young, Contemptuous yet unhandsome", as
Donne unkindly described it in his Third Satire) de-
manded of its adherents action, and heroic action at that.
Life was a fight, and an unceasing one till death. At the
very end of the first part of the *Pilgrim's Progress* Bunyan
recounts how Ignorance, ferried over the waters by Vain
Hope, came to the gates of Heaven claiming admittance.
Asked for his certificate, he cannot find it; and God
directs two angels who had escorted Christian and Hope-
ful through the gates to join the company of the blessed
"to bind him and have him away". They took him,
carried him through the air to the door that Christian
had seen in the side of the hill, and thrust him in. And
Bunyan adds, "Then I saw that there was a way to Hell,
even from the gates of Heaven, as well as from the City
of Destruction." So, to the Calvinist the least withdrawal
from the fight was fatal. William Haller, in his *Rise of
Puritanism*, has described the Puritan myth with its fierce
insistence on individual prowess, its democratic basis
(God being unsnobbish in his initial act of election), its
precise mapping out of the stages of sainthood achieved
by heroic Christian action, and its love of the metaphors
of way-faring and war-faring. In the Puritan warfare
Satan, himself a gigantic figure, was the prime enemy.

This Puritan myth is a specialised version of the myth of the superior man.

Unfortunately, there is no major work of art drawing its life from this specialised version of the myth at the time when puritanism in England held the strategic initiative: that is, roughly, during the first half of the seventeenth century. Puritan literary energy went into the sermon, into direct incitements to action, rather than into the less directly practical forms of literature; and later, when Milton wrote *Paradise Regained* and Bunyan the *Holy War*, not only had the wider myth of the superior man lost its vigour but the Puritans were the beaten party. When Milton and Bunyan used the theme of the battle with Satan they wrote more as individuals than as the instruments of a great pervasive myth.

To the very time when the Puritan myth most prevailed the origins of a counter-myth go back. The counter-myth did not exert its full sway till the beginning of the eighteenth century; and in its growth literature and nascent myth are interwoven: I mean that the literature may have contributed to the myth's formation; the opposite situation to that we found governing the Harrowing of Hell, where the myth took a complete shape before art and letters made use of it. With the double urge it is not surprising that the same writer could take either side. Thus we must not wonder if Milton at one time says:

> *And may at last my weary age*
> *Find out the peaceful hermitage,*
> *The hairy gown and mossy cell,*
> *Where I may sit and rightly spell*

> *Of every star that Heaven doth shew*
> *And every herb that sips the dew;*
> *Till old experience do attain*
> *To something like prophetic strain—*

and at another time,

> *I cannot praise a fugitive and cloistered virtue, unexercised and unbreathed, that never sallies out and sees her adversary, but slinks out of the race, where that immortal garland is to be run for, not without dust and heat.*

With this last passage from Milton I will leave the more hackneyed theme of aggression and take up the less hackneyed one of retirement.

# V. RETIREMENT

## 1. *The Initial Phase*

O NE of the great eighteenth-century myths was that of retirement from the busy world to a retreat, preferably in the country, from which to study the glories of God as revealed in nature and to contemplate the approach of death. It prevailed most strongly in the second quarter of the century; but its immediate ancestry was by then a hundred years old, and it continued to flourish for several more decades. The history of the concept from 1600 to 1760 has been traced with great learning and industry by Miss Maren-Sophie Røstvig of the University of Oslo, and in what follows I am much indebted to the two volumes of her book, the *Happy Man*.

The idea of retirement from the world is a human constant, but not always has it stirred enough people to achieve the intensity of a myth, while, when it has, the mythical form has varied. The monastic form the idea took in the Middle Ages is unlike the moralistic one it took in the eighteenth century. And one has only to look at the connotations of the word *retirement* at the present day to see how utterly lacking in mythological aura the concept can be. In an epoch when most people are forced to give up work at a certain age and proceed to enjoy that unromantically moderate and fixed affair, a pension, it is hard to invest the concept with the least emotion. Even if a man dodges compulsion by voluntary retirement before the age-limit, we have no predisposition to any emotions on the matter. We may hear the news that A has resigned his partnership and that he and his wife have found a nice flat in Chelsea to retire to, or that B has sold his prep school and retired to a modernised Tudor farm in the Cotswolds; but the only emotions aroused have to do with Chelsea and the Cotswolds: that they chose to retire before the usual age is entirely *their* affair and has no general or intrinsic interest. In fact, in our own day the prevailing climate of opinion is so set against the concept that only by rebelling against the social norm can a man revive and make others notice it. Thus the *Times* recently inserted in its middle page the news that

> *in the belief that "industrial civilization is built on false foundations—money and power", Mr W. E. W. Petter, the aircraft designer, is leaving Britain next week in search of a life of contemplation in the mountain foothills of Switzerland.*

The classic example of the same process is D. H. Lawrence, whose life from one side could be called a series of unsuccessful attempts to find the right place to retire to for the exercise of the particular forms of religion he came to profess. His most ambitious book, the *Plumed Serpent*, is indeed the story of a woman who, after various struggles, is supposed to succeed in the attempt. The story may not convince us, but there is no doubt about its theme and about the parallel it provides. The very struggles of Kate to get clear of her Mexican retreat can be matched by eighteenth-century accounts of the temptations suffered by the retired man in his country retreat to return to the bustle of the town. This is Lawrence's account of almost her last reluctance:

*Christmas was coming! The poinsettia reminded Kate of it.
Christmas! Holly-berries! England! Presents! Food! If she
hurried, she could be in England for Christmas. It felt so safe,
so familiar, so normal, the thought of Christmas at home, in
England, with her mother. And all the exciting things she
could tell to the people at home! And all the exciting gossip she
could hear! . . .*

"*How awful, Christmas with hibiscus and poinsettia! It
makes me long to see mistletoe among the oranges, in a fruiterer's
shop in Hampstead . . . to see the buses rolling on the mud in
Piccadilly on Christmas Eve, and the wet pavements crowded
with people under the brilliant shops.*"

During the age of aggression it could happen that a
superior man was banished the court, lost his outlet in
action, retired to the country, and proceeded to proclaim
how corrupt was the life he had left and how good was
his life of retreat. But any occasional poems that resulted,
like one of Wyatt's satires and Spenser's *Colin Clout's Come
Home Again*, are sour-grapes poems and not retirement
poems at all. However, they sometimes used classical
precedent, and it is this precedent, as followed and
developed in the early seventeenth century, that gener-
ated the literary form of what was ultimately to become
the retirement myth. It happened that certain classical
poems or passages advising retreat and contemplation of
the world from afar were much loved and dwelt on at
that time. Chief among these were Horace's lyric and
didactic utterances on the simple and moderate life, best
attained on a small country estate, Virgil's passionate
encomium of rural bliss in his *Georgics*, Lucretius's picture
of the impassive Epicurean watching from an eminence

the struggles of the mass of men below him, and one or two epigrams of Martial in praise of the simple life. All these were utter commonplaces, passages translated over and over again, words that had acquired a fixed place in the minds of all educated men. The Stoic retreated to the fortress of his self and kept the senseless traffic of the world at bay; Epicurus retired physically to his own garden to be able to live to himself. Here was classical precedent for a theory of life which, not thus supported, might in those still early days of the Reformation have been suspected of the taint of a still lingering monasticism. Granted that the urge to withdraw from the world is a constant in man and that it began now to reassert itself, it is not surprising if the more thoughtful and better educated used the growing fashion of seeking precedents in the classics to shape and justify that urge.

But the urge to retire was more religious than its classical precedent and insisted on going beyond it. This necessary process of sanctifying the pagan tradition was helped in England by the example of the immensely popular Polish poet, Mathias Casimir Sarbiewski or Sarbievius. Casimir, as he was usually called, was a Jesuit who published Horatian odes in Latin in 1625 and 1628 and earned through them a high European reputation. He admired Horace, but went beyond him in two ways. First, he had a more vivid sensuous feeling for nature and, second, he thought that man could use nature as a means of communion with God in a way quite foreign to the Roman stoic. There is easy access for English readers to samples of Casimir through Henry Vaughan's beautiful translations of seven of his odes. In these you get, first, sentiments purely devotional, next, sentiments hardly distinguishable from the conventionally classical versions of retirement, and, last, the theme, more apt to the present context, of the approach to God through nature. Casimir's ode, IV, 15, dwelling on the "peevish weariness" of men today and their perpetual desire for change, is purely Horatian.

> *We change the air each year and scorn*
> *Those seats in which we first were born.*

Happiness, he continues, depends not on where we live but on ourselves.

> *But he whose constancy makes sure*
> *His mind and mansion, lives secure*
> *From such vain tasks, can dine and sup*
> *Where his old parents bred him up.*
> *Content, no doubt, most times doth dwell*
> *In country shades, or to some cell*
> *Confines itself; and can alone*
> *Make simple straw a royal throne.*

But Casimir also wrote a poem expressly directed against the worldly quietism of Horace's "Beatus ille qui procul negotiis . . ."; and this Vaughan has translated. The ode begins

> *Flaccus, not so! that worldly he*
> *Whom in the country's shade we see*
> *Ploughing his own fields seldom can*
> *Be justly styled the blessed man.*
> *That title only fits the saint.*

And Casimir goes on to describe how the truly blessed man finds God through the medium of nature.

# RETIREMENT

He in the evening, when on high
The stars shine in the silent sky,
Beholds th' eternal flames with mirth
And globes of light more large than Earth;
Then weeps for joy and through his tears
Looks at the fire-enamelled spheres,
Where with his Saviour he would be
Lifted above mortality. . . .
In the calm spring, when the Earth bears
And feeds on April's breath and tears,
His eyes, accustomed to the skies,
Find here fresh objects and, like spies
Or busy bees, search the soft flowers,
Contemplate the green fields and bowers,
Where he in veils and shades doth see
The back parts of the deity.
Then, sadly sighing, says, "Oh, how
These flowers with hasty, stretched heads grow
And strive for Heaven, but rooted here
Lament the distance with a tear!
The honeysuckles clad in white,
The rose in red, point to the light;
And the lillies, hollow and bleak,
Look as if they would something speak;
They sigh at night to each soft gale
And at the day-spring weep it all.
Shall I then only, wretched I,
Oppressed with earth on earth still lie?"
Thus speaks he to the neighbour trees,
And many sad soliloquies
To springs and fountains doth impart,
Seeking God with a longing heart.

I do not mean that without Casimir the notion of retirement would not have become one of the prevalent myths of the eighteenth century; I mean that it helped the predisposition towards the idea that raised it into the mythical realm.

The case for withdrawal derived a sudden access of strength from a political event: the end of the first phase of the Civil War in the defeat of the King's party in England. It was in this party rather than in the opposing Puritans that the urge to withdraw began to be felt; and now the Cavaliers were deprived of what had become their main outlet of activity. No wonder if the ideal of retirement was invested with powerful feelings and became for the beaten party a kind of myth.

Mankind has devised a number of ways of dealing with the bitter fact of military defeat. The least noble is to try to ignore it by using some kind of drug; the most noble, perhaps, is to decide that defeat is actually for the best, to immerse in the destructive element. That is how the Serbs dealt with their defeat at Kossovo. Far from seeking to ignore it they have made it the centre of their legends, feigning, for instance, in their ballads that before the battle a dove, sent by God from Jerusalem, asked King Lazarus whether he would choose victory and success in this life or defeat and glory in the next world; and he chose defeat. The English retirement myth of the middle of the seventeenth century was something between these two extremes. England had fallen on evil days, and the defeated side could now do nothing about it. The rational thing was to retire from active life to the country, where the soul could turn inward on itself and get closer to God by fostering the godlike element within it. There were of course degrees of piety in the act, sometimes, as with Vaughan, amounting to an almost ascetic fervour, sometimes nearer to the garden of Epicurus than to the cloister; but that retirement involved some degree of piety is beyond doubt. It was not mere evasion but the setting of life in another direction.

Miss Røstvig has compiled an impressive list of writers in pre-Restoration England who made retirement their theme; and though, through confinement to a single topic, she fails to avoid giving the impression that some of them were concerned with retirement to the exclusion of everything else, she has proved its ubiquity. If, fresh from reading her book, one turns, for instance, to the works of Vaughan, whom she makes much of, one begins by being sceptical. So much of Vaughan is purely devotional without any hint that retirement is the means of devotion, some of it is secular, much of it is personal and occasional. But in the end you have to agree that the theme is there after all and that it was indeed dear to his heart. The *Bee*, for instance, is heart-felt both in its references to the evils of the times and in its resolution that a rural retreat from them into the enduring truths of religion is the only proper course. There are times, as Elijah found, when the wilderness is the only fit abode.

> *When truth and piety are missed*
> *Both in the rulers and the priest;*
> *When pity is not cold but dead,*
> *And the rich eat the poor like bread;*
> *While factious heads with open coil*
> *And force first make, then share, the spoil;*
> *To Horeb then Elias goes*

*And in the desert grows the rose.*
*Hail crystal fountains and fresh shades,*
*Where no proud look invades,*
*No busy worldling hunts away*
*The sad retirer all the day!*
*Hail, happy, harmless solitude!*
*Our sanctuary from the rude*
*And scornful world; the calm recess*
*Of faith and hope and holiness!*

I have not the time to mention more than a few samples out of the wealth of the retirement poetry of the time of the Civil War. Vaughan, of whom I have said enough already, was typical in having fought on the King's side and then in retiring to his country estate. Benlowes did the same; and I single him out because of his interesting references to the war in the midst of his retirement verse. Benlowes's long poem, *Theophila*, is one of those poems a discreet anthology of whose parts amounts to much more than the whole. It contains striking phrases and can be read with pleasure over a few short stretches. Being unoriginal, containing much plagiarism, it shows the direction of current taste with admirable clarity; and its culmination in two final cantos on the virtues of retirement indicates the genuine hold that this theme had on the minds and imaginations of one section of the community. These cantos indeed contain all that is most typical of the retirement poetry of the middle of the seventeenth century. Benlowes, a country gentleman and at one time a Catholic, became an ardent Anglican and Royalist, equally averse to Catholicism and Puritanism. He seems to have fought at Edgehill, and, when military activity was denied him, retired to his estate to live a life of pious retreat. He knew Casimir's poems and like him finds that the sensuous delight in natural things can lead to a closer walk with God. In spite of publishing his poem during the Commonwealth (1652) he dares to speak bitterly, if with discreet analogy, of the present plight of religion and then of his loyalty to the martyr-king:

> *Lord, guide thy church, which interests impair.*
> > *Who without knowledge factious are*
> *They little mind the flock, so they the fleece may share.*

> *Why climbed they else the pulpit, as Lot's brother,*
> > *With fire in one hand, knife i' th' other?*
> *'Twas vip'rous Nero slew his own indulgent mother.*

Anyhow the times are bad, and withdrawal is the only policy.

> *Thus go we like the heroes of old Greece,*
> > *In quest of more than golden fleece;*
> *Retreating to sweet shades our scattered thoughts we piece.*

And there is good precedent for such withdrawal: Charles V, Moses, John the Baptist, Christ himself. In his withdrawal the poet walks forth at dawn to enjoy the flowers and the birds' song, but the hoarse murmur of the stream sounds like a lament and reminds him of the woes of his country.

> *Edgehill with bones looked white, with blood looked red,*
> > *Mazed at the number of the dead:*
> *A theme for tears in unborn eyes to be still shed.*

He then thinks of the royal martyr; and this thought, like his thoughts on nature, leads him to thoughts of God:

> *Such mental buds we from each object take*
> *And for Christ's spouse of them we make*
> *Spiritual wreaths.*

And the rest of the poem is in a mode of high and fantastic devotion.

Benlowes's poetry is minor poetry; and to pass from it to an acknowledged masterpiece reverses the usual order of approach. We read Shakespeare before we learn his setting in Elizabethan drama; we read Wordsworth in isolation before we learn that he is the heir of many eighteenth-century poems. Thus we read Marvell's *Garden* in an anthology, most likely, and think of it as unique. In a way, of course, it is; but it is also a typical "retirement" poem, embodying the commonplaces of the kind: the futility of the crowd of the ambitious, the barren suffering of the lover, the innocence of the country retreat, its near recapture of the innocence of Paradise, and its virtue in promoting a state of spiritual exaltation. It is untypical in its exceptional poetic quality and in its having for author not a Royalist but a Parliamentarian. This second oddity can be readily explained. Marvell was anything but a mere partisan even though he took part in practical politics. He had a capacious mind that grasped the whole of an issue, that could, up to a point, be on both sides at once. He was able to be friends with Lovelace, a poet very much on the opposite side. Then one must remember that Marvell wrote the *Garden* while living at Appleton House and that to Appleton the great Lord Fairfax, Parliamentary Commander-in-Chief, re-

tired, when he could not longer co-operate with Cromwell. Fairfax was related by marriage to the other side,
and in some ways found himself retired much as were
some of his kin by marriage. The setting in which Marvell
then found himself was not unfavourable to the kind of
poetry to which the *Garden* belongs.

What separates the *Garden* from all other poems of its
kind is its speed and concentration. The recurrent subjects of the futile din of the town, the vanity of the
ambitions pursued there, capable of endless amplification,
are compressed into the first six lines, lines heavy with
meaning through the pregnancy of the words themselves
and the significant emphasis with which some of them fall.

> *How vainly men themselves amaze*
> *To win the palm, the oak, the bays,*
> *And their uncessant labours see*
> *Crown'd from some single herb or tree,*
> *Whose short and narrow-verged shade*
> *Does prudently their toils upbraid.*

(Here *amaze* bears its original meaning of *confuse* or *perplex*.)
Marvell here is saying that, fundamentally, these men,
even if they do gain distinction as soldiers, statesmen, or
poets (*palm, oak, bays*), are confused, for they are mere
specialists (emphasis on *single*); and this specialisation is a
reproach, a standing criticism of what they have done.
The word *prudently* pours cold water on their pretensions.
And the implication, abundantly fulfilled in the rest of
the poem, is that these quests of distinction have been
pursued at the price of forgetting the real quest of man:
that of himself. This vital compression which the first
lines illustrate is maintained throughout a poem that has

been annotated so abundantly as to make any further comment on it here impertinent.

Marvell's *Garden*, then, is the poetic crown of those years in the seventeenth century when the notion of retirement was most strongly reinforced by politics and religion, when it achieved its highest pitch of vitality, when it came nearest to being a myth. And it may properly be asked at this point whether any of the literature of retirement at this time has added to the country's later stock of poetical mythology. The answer must be that it did not. The bulk of literature that exploits the theme is minor literature. Of two greater poets who come into the picture one, Vaughan, is not popularly associated with retirement at all but with childhood, and the other, Marvell, was known but fitfully till the twentieth century and his verse has hardly had time to mature into myth. The one bit of literature of retirement that may be allowed a mythical aura antedates the most vital period; it is Milton's *Il Penseroso*. Milton's meditative man in his tower did indeed manage to enter the popular imagination; and it is natural for Yeats, describing his house in time of civil war, to write:

> *A winding stair, a chamber arched with stone,*
> *A grey stone fireplace with an open hearth,*
> *A candle and written page.*
> Il Penseroso's *Platonist toiled on*
> *In some like chamber.*

## 2. *Transitional Phase*

With the Restoration the literature of retirement experienced the slackening of "enthusiasm" common to

the time. Cowley's essays written under the Common-
wealth, with their tamer, less strenuously religious note,
anticipate the change. They were greatly read well into
the eighteenth century and they looked forward to that
"innocent Epicureanism" that Miss Røstvig considers the
mark of the retirement literature of the latter part of the
seventeenth century.

One of the most attractive minor figures among these
innocent Epicureans is John Norris of Bemerton. In doctrine he was a late product of Cambridge Platonism, a
disciple of Henry More; but his Platonic strain alternates
with the Epicurean one rather than is fused with it. In
his retirement verse he is the follower of Lucretius, contemplating in serene solitude the struggles of the remote
mob. He is a minor poet with a small range but he has a
decided and agreeable character; and that character consists in his combining the current lucidity of the Restoration with that power to suggest the actual processes of
thought which is one of the great attractions of Donne.
Of course, Donne was as much an artist as the poets whose
smoothness suggests prolonged artistry; only, part of his
art went into creating the appearance of his thinking
things out in the very act of composition. Of Donne's
followers it was Herbert who, speaking in a quieter and
more winning voice, best inherited his peculiar gift. Norris
in his little way is the genuine follower of these two greater
men. He is indeed one of the minor poets who deserve
more attention than they get. He does not figure in the
*Oxford Book of English Verse*, but there are two good
samples of his work in the *Oxford Book of Seventeenth
Century Verse*. I quote his poem, *Retirement*, not because
there are not others that would illustrate his capacities as

well but because it is one of those two samples and can be easily found by those who may be interested in him.

### The Retirement

*Well, I have thought on't, and I find*
*This busy world is nonsense all;*
*I here despair to please my mind,*
*Her sweetest honey is so mix'd with gall.*
*Come then, I'll try how 'tis to be alone,*
*Live to myself a while, and be my own.*

*I've tried, and bless the happy change;*
*So happy, I could almost vow*
*Never from this retreat to range,*
*For sure I ne'er can be so blest as now.*
*From all th'allays of bliss I here am free:*
*I pity others, and none envy me.*

*Here in this shady lonely grove*
*I sweetly think my hours away,*
*Neither with business vex'd nor love,*
*Which in the world bear such tyrannic sway:*
*No tumults can my close apartment find,*
*Calm as those seats above which know no storm nor wind.*

*Let plots and news embroil the state—*
*Pray what's that to my books and me?*
*Whatever be the kingdom's fate,*
*Here I am sure t' enjoy a monarchy.*
*Lord of myself, accountable to none,*
*Like the first man in Paradise, alone.*

*While the ambitious vainly sue*
*And of the partial stars complain,*
*I stand upon the shore and view*
*The mighty labours of the distant main.*
*I'm flushed with silent joy and smile to see*
*The shafts of fortune still drop short of me.*

*Th' uneasy pageantry of state,*
*And all the plagues of thought and sense*
*Are far removed; I'm placed by fate*
*Out of the road of all impertinence.*
*Thus, though my fleeting life runs swiftly on,*
*'Twill not be short because 'tis all my own.*

Of this age, though usually allotted to the next century,
are the retirement poems of Anne, Countess of Winchelsea, and of Pomfret. Colonel and Anne Finch, later
to become Earl and Countess of Winchelsea, devoted to
James II, retired in distress to the country when he was
driven from the throne. They were thus in much the
same case as were Benlowes and his like during the Civil
War. As a Non-Juror Colonel Finch was debarred further
service for the government; and he and his wife were
ultimately given a home in the house of the then earl, a
young man whom Colonel Finch was destined to succeed.
There they belonged to a circle of like-minded, cultured
High Churchmen which included Bishop Ken, now
known for the tradition of his saintliness and as the author
of two of the best loved English hymns. It was in these
circumstances that towards the end of the seventeenth
century Anne Finch wrote one of her well remembered
poems, *The Petition for an Absolute Retreat*. It is in the
*Oxford Book of Eighteenth Century Verse* (presumably because

it was not published till 1713), but in a truncated form, the omissions including the moving topical passage about the authoress's mental prostration when the Stuarts were expelled. Ardelia in the passage is what she called herself in her verse, while Arminda is the Countess of Thanet, one of her chief supports in the evil days after 1688.

> *When a helpless vine is found*
> *Unsupported on the ground,*
> *Careless all the branches spread,*
> *Subject to each haughty tread,*
> *Bearing neither leaves nor fruit,*
> *Living only in the root,*
> *Back reflecting let me say:*
> *So the sad Ardelia lay,*
> *Blasted by a storm of fate*
> *Felt through all the British state;*
> *Fall'n, neglected, lost, forgot,*
> *Dark oblivion all her lot;*
> *Faded till Arminda's love,*
> *Guided by the powers above,*
> *Warmed anew her drooping heart*
> *And life diffused through every part.*

The line "living only in the root" strikes me as a swift and (poetically) direct expression of a most sincere piece of personal feeling. And the poem as a whole belongs not to the new nature poetry of the eighteenth century but to the authentic seventeenth-century poetry of retirement. And the ending with its passionate tone of devotion approximates it rather to the enthusiastic poetry of the mid century than to the Epicureanism of the contemporary poetry of retreat.

# RETIREMENT

*Fitly might the life of man*
*Be indeed esteemed a span,*
*If no other joys he knew*
*Than what round about him grew.*
*But as those who stars would trace*
*From a subterranean place*
*Through some engine lift their eyes*
*To the outward, glorious, skies;*
*So the immortal spirit may,*
*When descended to our clay,*
*From a rightly governed frame*
*View the height from whence she came,*
*To her paradise be caught*
*And things unutterable taught.*
*Give me, then, in that retreat,*
*Give me, O indulgent fate,*
*For all pleasures left behind,*
*Contemplations of the mind.*
*Let the fair, the gay, the vain,*
*Courtship and applause obtain;*
*Let th'ambitious rule the earth;*
*Let the giddy fool have mirth;*
*Give the Epicure his dish—*
*Every one their several wish—*
*Whilst my transports I employ*
*On that more extensive joy*
*When all Heaven shall be surveyed*
*From those windings and that shade.*

There is not a word here that does not conform to the retirement myth, now so firmly established and, one would think, ready to go stale. Yet that myth, far from forcing Anne Finch to the frigid and the inert, gave her the means of expressing a singularly fresh set of personal feelings.

John Pomfret's *The Choice*, though written in the seventeenth century, is the first poem printed in the *Oxford Book of Eighteenth Century Verse*. And its position there is apt, since it is a prospective poem and the perfect foretaste of the new age. It marks, as surely as the *Spectator* does, the emergence into influence of the middling man. It does indeed treat of retirement, but of a retirement most unlike the spirituality of a Vaughan or the refined and aristocratic Epicureanism of Norris of Bemerton. Pomfret may pretend to a virtuous moderation but what he ends by preaching is a most thorough feathering of a solid middle-class nest.

> *I'd have a clear and competent estate*
> *That I might live gentilely, but not great.*

In other words he would go for solid comfort and not mind about the trimmings.

> *I'd have a little vault, but always stored*
> *With the best wines each vintage could afford.*

When you come to think of it, the moderate size of the cellar, provided it is always stocked, makes not the slightest difference to the actual drinking. True, he would make moderate use of this good wine, but, we always feel, on the strictly utilitarian ground that you get more out of it thus used. In many ways *The Choice* is a most ridiculous poem, and especially in its relentless iteration of the theme of the mean and of balance. The author's house will strike a compromise between town and country, being "near some fair town", and of course it will be neither big nor small. He will have two special friends, of course one to balance the other. And so on and so on right through to the end. Yet *The Choice* is not despicable as poetry. It falls pleasantly on the ear and it is carefully and conscientiously wrought, and civilised in a middle-class way.

### 3. Climax

Pomfret's appeal to the middling reader shows something that took place in the last years of the seventeenth century: the myth of retirement ceased to be confined to one section of the community. The reason of course lay with the settlement of 1689. When the Dissenters ceased to be either the militant conquerors or the victims of persecution, the edge of their aggressive temper was taken off and they began to share in the interests of their late enemies. Millenarian hopes were abandoned, and it was possible to sympathise with the notion of quiet and pious retreat from the noisy world. Miss Røstvig points out that one of the main transitional figures in this process was the great dissenting divine, Dr Watts, who was familiar with the retirement poetry of Casimir, Cowley, and Norris and whose odes, now neglected, add to the tradition. By the time of the *Spectator* the myth of retirement was the property of all educated sections of the community.

Not only did the myth extend the range of its public at the end of the seventeenth century; it acquired a new and powerful source of vitality in the great advances of science made at that time. The great scientists were mostly pious; and the idea grew up that one of the readiest means of access to God was through the study, now immensely enlarged, of the works of God, whether in their huge manifestations in the sky or in their minute ones of the insect world. These passages from John Ray's *Wisdom of God manifested in the Works of Creation* (1691) are entirely typical of the prevalent belief:

> *That the fixed stars are innumerable may thus be made out: Those visible to the naked eye are by the least account acknowledged to be above a thousand. . . . Besides these there have been incomparably more detected and brought to light by the telescope, the Milky Way being found to be . . . nothing but great companies and swarms of minute stars singly invisible but by reason of their proximity mingling and confounding their lights and appearing like lucid clouds. And it's likely that, had we more perfect telescopes, many thousands more might be discovered; and yet, after all, an incredible multitude remain by reason of their immense distance beyond all ken by the best telescopes that could possibly be invented or polished by the wit and hand of an angel.*
>
> *What can we infer from all this? If the number of creatures be so exceeding great, how great, nay immense, must needs be the power and wisdom of him who formed them all! For . . . as it argues and manifests more skill by far in an artificer to be able to frame both clocks and watches and pumps and mills and granadoes and rockets than he could display in making but one of those sorts of engines; so the Almighty discovers more of his wisdom in forming such a vast multitude of different sorts of creatures, and all with admirable and irreprovable art, than if he had created but a few, for this declares the greatness and unbounded capacity of his understanding.*

And later in his book Ray says that God made so many creatures both to display his power and wisdom and to exercise man's faculty of contemplation. The passages quoted give the current doctrine of the immense variety of God's works, but, balancing it, is the joyful belief that Newton's work in simplifying the laws of nature added powerfully to man's conceptions of the majesty of God. The new picture of God as majestically simple in his means and infinitely complex in his results was felt to be superior to any previous picture. Finally it was thought that this new picture was best perceived not in an urban setting but in country retirement.

Newton's influence on the general public reached its height in the quarter century after his death in 1727. And it is at this time that the myth of retirement most prevailed. Not only did it now enter literature most widely but it incited people to action; it really induced people to take the practical step of exchanging town for country quiet.

Can it be said that in this age the myth received some culminating literary embodiment? Miss Røstvig seems to think that it does so in Thomson's *Seasons*. Here I cannot follow her. It is indeed true that Thomson was open to the full impact of the current cult of Newton. Shortly before Newton's death he became a tutor in a newly founded academy in Little Tower Street in London which specialised in popularising the new science and had on its staff men competent to do so; and, when Newton died, Thomson interrupted his work on the *Seasons* to write his splendid poem *Sacred to the Memory of Sir Isaac Newton*, which shows not only a good popular knowledge of Newton's chief scientific discoveries but signs that

Thomson knew him personally and that the grief he professes was more than conventional.[1] And if you choose the right passages you can make a good case for the *Seasons* being a poem of retirement. Taken as a whole I do not find it to be of that kind. The old idea of Thomson's being above all a descriptive poet seems to me the right one; and the descriptive passages in his poem count for more than any prevailing ideas that are supposed to join them together. For myself I think that the myth of retirement finds its culminating embodiments in two places: in landscape gardening, on which Miss Røstvig has an admirable chapter, and in a single novel, which she does not mention.

On landscape gardening I shall say little. It is a topic more complicated and more important than is usually recognised. Some of its manifestations are major works of art, and we shall not do the eighteenth century justice unless we take them fully into account. How can we estimate what that century was good for without taking into account, for instance, the Earl of Leicester's park that surrounds Holkham Hall in Norfolk? The total conception of it is majestic in the extreme and it allows for a huge range of detail. It can fitly be compared with the literary kind of epic. But Holkham takes one beyond the topic of retirement; and the present point is that the new type of gardening that began to prevail in the early years of the eighteenth century was closely associated with the retirement myth. It is well enough known that at this time taste reacted from the formal, enclosed, rectangular

[1] See Douglas Grant, *The Poet of the Seasons* (London 1951), 71-2. Grant thinks that Thomson knew Newton personally though the mathematician, James Stirling, who also taught at the academy.

kind of garden to one which mimicked nature and favoured large prospects appealing to the romantic imagination. The classic enunciation of the theory on which such practice was founded is one of Addison's series of essays on the pleasures of the imagination in the *Spectator*, No. 414. In it he says:

> *There is something more bold and masterly in the rough careless strokes of nature than in the nice touches and embellishments of art. The beauties of the most stately garden or palace lie in a narrow compass, the imagination immediately runs them over and requires something else to gratify her; but in the wild fields of nature the sight wanders up and down without confinement and is fed with an infinite number of images, without any certain stint or number.*

Nevertheless, nature is most delightful not when it is most disordered but when it gives the sense of having been touched by art. Contrariwise,

> *if the products of nature rise in value according as they more or less resemble those of art, we may be sure that artificial works receive a greater advantage from their resemblance of such as are natural.*

As I say, this principle is well enough known. It is less known that, as Miss Røstvig demonstrates, the principle that a garden should imitate the great expanses of nature derives from the kind of sentiment contained in the passage I have quoted from John Ray on the immensity of God's works. As the soul of man expanded by contemplating that immensity, so rural retirement and the garden, already propitious for the soul's good, would be most so, not in an enclosed and formal, but in a natural and expanded setting.

That the eighteenth century did indeed put landscape gardening in so solemn a context is amply proved by the writings on the subject. An instructive and amusing example of these is Stephen Switzer's *Nobleman, Gentleman, and Gardener's Recreation*, published in 1715, and re-issued with additions under the title of *Ichnographia Rustica* in 1718. Switzer, from the way he writes, was obviously a self-educated man and a practical gardener. Of himself he said, "I have tasted both rough and smooth from the best business and books to the meanest labours of the scythe, spade, and wheelbarrow." He is thus all the more likely to represent current opinion faithfully. In enlarging on God's handiwork in nature he places his climax in the country seat of an English gentleman.

> *But of all works of creation none calls for our attention more than the superficies of the earth, the work of the third day: the beautifulness there is in the prospect of it; the excellent uses and variety therein are studies and speculations that excel all others. And amidst all, that of a country seat distributed with judgement may be accounted one of the greatest.*

Here, as elsewhere in Switzer, there is an uneasy feeling that he was on the lookout for orders; but, ingenuousness of expression apart, there is no doubt that his high sentiments were those of many of his patrons and of his readers. Needless to say, the word *retirement* occurs in his books.

The great literary work inspired by the myth of retirement is Defoe's *Robinson Crusoe*. True, it differs from most other embodiments of the myth in not insisting on the country as the proper setting for the contemplation that retirement should afford. Crusoe's father, who preaches the virtues of a life free from excessive toil and ambition was a merchant living in retirement at York. On the other hand the island to which God compels Crusoe to retire compensates by the extremity of its solitude. Still, it is the quiet and loneliness of the island rather than any lesson its natural beauties convey that are the pre-requisites of Crusoe's spiritual rehabilitation. I have argued in my *Epic Strain in the English Novel* that this is the book's main theme in spite of the doubts cast on Defoe's char-acter and consequent suspicions of insincerity. I do not wish to repeat myself on *Robinson Crusoe*, that is on the first part; but I would not leave Defoe without making more emphatic the plea that he did in fact embody the retirement myth. And this I can do by summarising an unfamiliar episode: unfamiliar because it occurs in the little read second part of the same book, near the end.

On his last journey back from his island with his partner, Robinson travels through Japan, China, and Siberia. Caught by the Russian winter, the travellers put up at Tobolsk, the Siberian capital. Defoe's peculiar art is at its height when he describes all the circumstances, for it is impossible to doubt that the narrator is speaking from personal experience and is recounting something that actually happened to him. Now Tobolsk was the receptacle of distinguished political exiles, and among them was a certain prince who had once held high office under the Czar. He and Crusoe become familiar, and Crusoe tells him about the little kingdom he has estab-lished on his island, where there is no trouble, Crusoe being sole owner and absolute but entirely beloved despot. The prince says he envies Crusoe, who is far happier in his modest way than the great Czar himself, and then goes on to talk of his own predicament as a banished man; and he asserts

*that he found more felicity in the retirement he seemed to be banished to than ever he found in the highest authority he enjoyed in the court of his master the Czar: that the height of human wisdom was to bring our tempers down to our circumstances and to make a calm within under the weight of the greatest scorns without. When he first came hither, he said, he used to tear the hair from his head and the clothes from his back, as others had done before him: but a little time and consideration had made him look into himself as well as round him to things without: that he found the mind of man, if it was but once brought to reflect upon the state of universal life and how little this world was concerned with its true felicity, was perfectly capable of making a felicity for itself, fully satisfying to itself and suitable to its own best ends and desires with but very little assistance from the world; that air to breathe in, food to sustain life, clothes for warmth, and liberty for exercise in order to health completed in his opinion all that the world could do for us: and though the greatness, the authority, the riches, and the pleasures which some enjoyed in the world and which he had enjoyed his share of, had much in them that was agreeable to us, yet he observed that all those things chiefly gratified the coarsest of our affections. . . . If I know anything of myself I would not now go back, though the Czar my master should call me and reinstate me in my former grandeur; I say, I would no more go back to it than I believe my soul, when it shall be delivered from this prison of the body and has had a taste of the*

*glorious state beyond life, would come back to the gaol of flesh
and blood it is now enclosed in and leave heaven to deal in the
dirt and crime of human affairs.*

Crusoe congratulates the prince on this victory over himself but proceeds to insinuate a doubt and asks whether
"if the door of your liberty was opened, would you not
take hold of it to deliver yourself from this exile?"

*"Hold," he said, "your question is subtle and requires some
serious just distinctions to give it a sincere answer; and I'll
give it you from the bottom of my heart. Nothing that I know
of in this world would move me to deliver myself from this state
of banishment except these two: first, the enjoyment of my
relations and, secondly, a little warmer climate. But I protest
to you that to go back to the pomp of the court, the glory, the
power, the hurry of a minister of state; the wealth, the gaiety,
and the pleasures, that is to say, follies of a courtier; if my
master should send word this moment, that he restores me to all
he banished me from, I protest, if I know myself at all, I would
not leave this wilderness, these deserts, and these frozen lakes
for the palace at Moscow."*

After the long bitter winter, superbly described, Crusoe
prepares for his journey to Archangel and his final voyage
thence home. He is to take an unusual route by which it
would be possible for a political exile to evade the guards,
who would catch him if he attempted passage by what
were deemed the only ways of escape. Crusoe asks his
friend the prince if this possibility for his escape were not
a heaven-sent opportunity. Confronted with this opportunity the unfortunate prince is dreadfully torn in mind,
but at length he makes his decision and tells Crusoe that

his offer, made in all good faith, may be anything but heaven-sent:

> *How do you know that, instead of a summons from Heaven, it may not be a feint of another instrument, representing in all the alluring colours to me, the show of felicity as a deliverance which may in itself be my snare and tends directly to my ruin? Here I am free from the temptation of returning to my former miserable greatness; there I am not sure but that all the seeds of pride, ambition, avarice, and luxury, which I know remain in nature, may revive and take root, and, in a word, again overwhelm me; and then the happy prisoner, who you now see master of his soul's liberty, shall be the miserable slave of his own senses in the full of all personal liberty. Dear sir, let me remain in this blessed confinement, banished from the crimes of life, rather than purchase a show of freedom at the expense of the liberty of my reason and at the expense of the future happiness which now I have in my view but shall then, I fear, quickly lose sight of; for I am but flesh, a man, a mere man, have passions and affections as likely to possess and overthrow me as any man. Oh, be not my friend and my tempter both together!*
>
> *If I was surprised before, I was quite dumb now and stood silent, looking at him; and, indeed, admired at what I saw. The struggle in his soul was so great that though the weather was extremely cold, it put him into a most violent sweat, and I found he wanted to give vent to his mind; so I said a word or two, that I would leave him to consider of it and wait on him again; and then I withdrew to my own apartment.*

The end is in keeping with the innocently homiletic and quite unsatirical tone of the whole episode. In two hours the prince returns in near composure. He declines the offer, recognises the kindness that prompted it, and gives Crusoe a handsome parting present.

What are we to make of the episode? It is a pure embodiment of the retirement myth, including, what I did not mention, an essential part of it, namely the presence of one or two kindred spirits to prevent the retirer's undue loneliness. In substance it is the tritest contemporary moralising; and a reader whom it left cold might reasonably accuse Defoe of pandering cynically to the tastes of lower middle-class pietism. But I believe the reader should not be left cold, for the episode is full of living detail (as when the prince confesses to two real deprivations: the company of his relations and a little warmer climate), that shows that Defoe was swallowed up by his theme, that imaginatively he identified himself with it. The prince's words are not second-hand sermon stuff but flow straight from his heart, raising his theme to a height above any treatment of it in the verse of the age.

In ordinary esteem Defoe does not rank as the culminating embodier of the retirement myth, because the great majority of readers confine their view of the man Robinson Crusoe to that of the practical man, the pioneer; they refuse to look on him also as the man who wilfully disregarded God's warnings to go back on the thoughtless life he has been leading and who was punished (but also blessed) by an enforced solitude in which he may find himself and save his soul. And in their refusal they astonish me by their blindness. All one can hope is that future readers will see with other eyes and that Defoe will be given the credit of having given the retirement myth its supreme embodiment.

### 4. Retrospect

Miss Røstvig thinks that retirement literature suffered a decline after about the year 1760; and this opinion is confirmed by the tone of one of the few masterpieces of the kind, Cowper's *Retirement*, published in 1782 as part of *Table Talk* and the best poem in that collection. Here Cowper is critical and bantering as well as solemn and pious, looking backwards or taking stock rather than seeking to promote. It will serve nicely as the epilogue to this section.

Cowper's poem contains no literary criticism. It is moral and it criticises classes of people. Apart from a brief reference to Pope's *Windsor Forest* and Thomson's *Seasons* it quite ignores the literature of retirement. It begins by referring to a social fact: that there has been an imperative fashion to retire from the town to the peace of the country. And it proceeds to inquire what in sober actuality the fashion amounts to:

> *Hackneyed in business, wearied at that oar*
> *Which thousands, once fast chained to, quit no more*
> *But which, when life at ebb runs weak and low,*
> *All wish, or seem to wish, they could forego;*
> *The statesman, lawyer, merchant, man of trade,*
> *Pants for the refuge of some rural shade.*

And Cowper concedes that genuine retirement to the country is a noble thing.

> *Happy, if full of days—but happier far,*
> *If, ere we yet discern life's evening star—*

*Sick of the service of the world, that feeds*
*Its patient drudges with dry chaff and weeds,*
*We can escape from Custom's idiot sway*
*To serve the Sovereign we were born to obey.*

And then Cowper shows himself the heir of Ray and
Newton in the lines that follow:

*Then sweet to muse upon his skill displayed*
*(Infinite skill) in all that he has made!*
*To trace in Nature's most minute design*
*The signature and stamp of power divine,*
*Contrivance intricate, expressed with ease,*
*Where unassisted sight no beauty sees,*
*The stately limb and lubricated joint*
*Within the small dimensions of a point,*
*Muscle and nerve miraculously spun,*
*His mighty work, who speaks and it is done,*
*Th'invisible, in things scarce seen revealed,*
*To whom an atom is an ample field.*

And to that inheritance he adds the note of religion,
different indeed from the mysticism of Vaughan, but not
less acutely felt. The basic justification of retirement is
for Cowper that it is more propitious than the worldly
life to the only task that ultimately is worth anything.

*To limit thought, by nature prone to stray*
*Wherever freakish Fancy points the way;*
*To bid the pleadings of Self-love be still,*
*Resign our own and seek our Maker's will;*
*To spread the page of Scripture and compare*
*Our conduct with the laws engraven there;*

*To measure all that passes in the breast,*
*Faithfully, fairly, by that sacred test;*
*To dive into the secret deeps within,*
*To spare no passion and no favorite sin*
*And search the themes, important above all:*
*Ourselves, and our recovery from our fall.*

Once a man has faced this task, all sorts of pleasures, sober indeed but exalted or elegant, are not denied him. If he is a poet he will find in nature his most congenial material. And the poet is the first of the different types of men whom Cowper proceeds now to measure by the standard that true retirement exacts. One type that is prone to seek comfort or rather to indulge himself in the country is the lover, and Cowper says that this is the very worst place for him. It tempts him to indulge his mood of adoration; and an active life is the better means of turning profitless adoration to rational affection. The next type is the victim of a mental breakdown, usually ordered by the physician to the country. Cowper, a recent victim himself, knows that the country effects nothing one way or the other.

*Man is a harp, whose chords elude the sight,*
*Each yielding harmony, disposed aright;*
*The screws reversed (a task which, if he please,*
*God in a moment executes with ease)*
*Ten thousand thousand strings at once go loose,*
*Lost, till he tune them, all their power and use.*
*Then neither heathy wilds, nor scenes as fair*
*As ever recompensed the peasant's care,*
*Nor soft declivities with tufted hills,*
*Nor view of waters turning busy mills . . .*

*Can call up life into his faded eye,*
*That passes all he sees unheeded by.*

There follows a section on the statesman who, nauseated
with responsibility, decides to settle in his ancestral estate
and pass his days in ease. But he has no resources in himself and soon exhausts the fund of amusement he finds at
hand, till in the end he

*feels, while grasping at his faded joys,*
*A secret thirst of his renounced employs.*
*He chides the tardiness of every post,*
*Pants to be told of battles won and lost,*
*Blames his own indolence, observes, though late,*
*'Tis criminal to leave a sinking state,*
*Flies to the levee, and, received with grace,*
*Kneels, kisses hands, and shines again in place.*

Superficially, this satirical account is much like Pope but
actually it does not compete. It lacks Pope's fierce
astringency, it is poetry of a much lower temperature,
but it makes up for this lack by its perfect clarity of
vision; and the very coolness and elegance of the satire,
so gentle and so unsparing, renders it in its own way
supremely effective.

Next there is the citizen who, thinking he is retiring
from the town, patronises the new ribbon-development.

*Suburban villas, highway-side retreats,*
*That dread th'encroachment of our growing streets;*
*Tight boxes neatly sashed and in a blaze*
*With all a July sun's collected rays*
*Delight the citizen, who, gasping there,*
*Breathes clouds of dust and calls it country air. . . .*

> *There, prisoned in a parlour snug and small,*
> *Like bottled wasps upon a southern wall,*
> *The man of business and his friends compressed*
> *Forget their labours.*

And there is always the traffic on the turnpike road for
diversion. Then there are those who rush to the seaside.
And then there is the impoverished landowner who hates
the country but is forced to live in it because he cannot
afford the pleasures of the town. And Cowper sums up
by saying:

> *Thus some retire to nourish hopeless woe;*
> *Some seeking happiness not found below;*
> *Some to comply with humour and a mind*
> *To social scenes by nature disinclined;*
> *Some swayed by fashion, some by deep disgust;*
> *Some self-impoverished and because they must;*
> *But few that court retirement are aware*
> *Of half the toils they must encounter there . . .*
> *'Tis easy to resign a toilsome place*
> *But not to manage leisure with a grace.*

Mere idle dreaming will not do; and Cowper reverts to
his assertion that only a man at peace with heaven can
stand the exactions of the retired life. He ends his poem
by saying what are the legitimate amusements of the man
thus qualified to retire. Books of course, but not those
of the philosophic scoffers, and

> *Not those of learned philologists, who chase*
> *A panting syllable through time and space,*
> *Start it at home and hunt it in the dark,*
> *To Gaul, to Greece, and into Noah's ark.*

They must be the genuine classics of learning or imagination. Then there is the society of the right kind of friend, manly, sympathetic, urbane, the study of nature, gardening, botanising, music, painting, and Cowper ends:

> *Me poetry (or rather notes that aim*
> *Feebly and vainly at poetic fame)*
> *Employs, shut out from more important views,*
> *Fast by the banks of the low-winding Ouse;*
> *Content if thus sequestered I may raise*
> *A monitor's, though not a poet's praise;*
> *And while I teach an art too little known—*
> *To close life wisely—may not waste my own.*

Where Cowper differs from the other, earlier, writers I have spoken of in this section is that, whereas they assumed as axiomatic the virtues of the retired life, he coolly asks what in actual fact it amounts to. And he concludes that it is a difficult life suited to a small minority and that its cult has produced a lot of pretence and hypocrisy. His tone is much that of Ovid at the beginning of his *Art of Love*, a poem dealing with the technique of illegitimate philandering. Don't expect an easy time, says Ovid; the art I'm dealing with is really pretty thankless; you must be prepared for much hard work to produce even a meagre result. However, if you insist on embarking on this unrewarding pastime, I will instruct you on the method of pursuing it. Cowper, for all his English Evangelicanism, shows an elegance of the critical spirit that we associate with the Latin countries: that he was able to turn it onto the myth of retirement proves that the days of the myth were over.

## VI. LIBERTY, OR 1066 AND ALL THAT

At the age of thirteen I spent a term at the Collège Cantonal at Lausanne. During one of the lessons the teacher suddenly asked me what quality or right the English valued most. In instantaneous reaction I answered "liberty". Justice, piety, kindliness—none of these virtues made the least stir in the repository of my mind—while "liberty" started up like a Jack-in-the-box. All unaware, in so speaking, I was airing part of the historical myth I had been brought up on and had accepted as axiomatic. The teacher did not go on and ask me how liberty came to be the great English characteristic; but, if he had, I should have repeated any relevant scraps of that strange anthology of events in English history which a few years ago were, and perhaps still are, most conveniently described as *1066 and All That*. This anthology does not cover the whole of the historical mythology of which liberty is the ruling motive, comprising only English or British history, for there was another anthology, leading up, it is true, to England, that covered the history of the whole of the western world. It is the wider myth that had the better literary results; but I must say something about the local myth first.

I have forgotten the name of the small book in which I first read the history of my country. But it had much in common with the most famous of all such volumes: *Little Arthur's History of England*. It is worth saying something about this very popular and influential book: a

book written with a lucidity and a singleness of mind that
no one attempting a similar book today could possibly
expect to rival. The authoress, Lady Callcott, was born
in 1785. She was the daughter of Rear-Admiral Dundas.
The *Dictionary of National Biography* records that her
governess had been acquainted with the Burneys, Rey-
nolds, and Johnson and that she often visited her uncle,
Sir David Dundas, at Richmond, where Rogers, Thomas
Campbell, and Lawrence were frequent guests. She was
thus the heir of the eighteenth century and the intimate
of men of similar inheritance. She married first Captain
Thomas Graham, R.N., lived in India and Valparaiso,
and was generally much travelled. Her second husband
was the artist, Sir Augustus Calcott. *Little Arthur's History
of England* was published in 1835. As one would expect
from her life and upbringing, the tone of her book is
pious, humane, and shows her entirely convinced of the
supremacy of her country and of the obligation of its
upper classes to serve it. On the title page there is the
picture of a desk, surmounted by a cushion, from which
hangs a scroll inscribed "Magna Charta". The scroll is
kept from falling off the cushion by its attachment to a
crown and sceptre above. On the ground, adjacent to the
bottom of the scroll, are the sword and scales of justice.
But it is Magna Charta that figures most prominently;
and Magna Charta meant "liberty".

   The text is in the main factual, for Lady Calcott did
not believe in the play-way in education. But it is
tendentious in making the course of English history lead
up to present felicity and it retails most of the legends
that compose "1066 and All That". History begins with
the Britons and includes woad and coracles. The Druids

have a chapter to themselves. Then came the Romans, who gave the Britons civilisation generally and schools in particular and who founded London, Bath, and York. Hengist and Horsa led the Saxon invasions, and we get a mention of Arthur. We hear of Angles and angels, the imposition of Peter's Pence, but above all that the Saxons were lovers of freedom, of which the existence of the Witenagemot was a sign. William the Conqueror was a stern ruler and instituted the curfew. Henry II never smiled again after the White Ship went down with his son. Much is made of Runnymede and Magna Charta: and so on and so on, with Joan of Arc a heroine and Richard III saying, "I will not dine till thy head is off". The single important matter in which *Little Arthur's History* differed from the one I was reared on is its treatment of the revolution of 1688. Although approving of it, Lady Calcott did not make it the supreme event to which all earlier advances of liberty led. Thus, in this particular instance, she diverged from the dominant mythological tradition of the eighteenth century. Otherwise she adhered to it faithfully.

What should strike one in considering English historical myth is how clearly the Whig myth, as it may be called for short, differs from the Elizabethan. As the climax of events the revolution of 1688 has supplanted the Battle of Bosworth and the establishment of the Tudors. King John, on the whole a bad man in both mythologies, was famous in the first for resisting the Pope, in the second for signing Magna Charta. Alfred has supplanted Arthur as the great hero of pre-Conquest England; and the whole complex of legends concerning Arthur deriving from Geoffrey Monmouth has been abolished in favour of

Saxon preludes to greater subsequent liberty. Strangely enough Joan of Arc was a bad woman in both myth-ologies, Shakespeare for instance making her a witch, and Goldsmith in his *History of England* making her a woman put up by the Dauphin to pose as inspired and the worker of miracles; in fact a fraud. It may be that she had to wait for Southey's poem on her before she could become the heroine she is in *Little Arthur's History*.

The complete story of how one mythology gave way to the other awaits its teller. The process happened in the seventeenth century; and parts of the story have received the attention of scholars. Here are a few details of the change. With the advent of the Stuarts it was impossible to maintain the sanctity that had invested the Battle of Bosworth and the accession of the Tudors. Men still praised Queen Elizabeth, and with redoubled fervour when they wished to vent their dislike of the Stuarts. But in the nature of things, with the Wars of the Roses now remote, they could no longer look on the Tudors as the house ordained by God to heal the terrible wounds of civil war. The Tudor myths became superannuated, and the Stuarts could not supply an acceptable replacement. The change in the rôle of King John happened as soon as the judges, headed by Coke, defended the Common Law against King James's claims to divine right in overriding it. The antiquaries, Selden and Spelman, then began digging into past history, and the signing and renewal of Magna Charta became important parts of their contro-versial armoury; from then on, men made more and more of them, till they became principal items in English political mythology.

The replacement of Britons by Saxons and Arthur by

Alfred is the subject of Miss R. F. Brinkley's *Arthurian Legend in the Seventeenth Century*. It is a very queer story, and largely because James I carried on the Arthurian affinities we associate with the Tudors. In view of the uncertainty about the succession it was politic to stress James's Arthurian descent through Margaret Tudor, daughter of Henry VII. But by a strange piece of luck this descent was not single, for when Fleance, son of Banquo, escaped the murderers hired by Macbeth, he fled to Wales and there he married Nesta, daughter of Griffith ap Llewelin, the last of the native Welsh princes. Their son, Walter, returned to Scotland, became Lord High Steward (whence the name of Stuart) and the ancestor of the Stuart house. Much was made of this double pedigree. And much would have continued unanimously to be made, if James had not provoked feeling by his claims to divine right. The same motive that led the antiquaries to revive interest in Magna Charta led them to study early English history: namely the need to find support in precedent for the limitation of the powers of the monarchy. There was nothing to be got out of the Arthurian lore of Geoffrey of Monmouth for this purpose, but the Saxons offered good material. Hence a relearning of the Anglo-Saxon tongue and the vaunting of councils of nobles and assemblies of wise men able to check the power of the king. As the century went on the two races, Celts and Saxons, became more and more involved in politics, the Royalists fostering the legends of the first and the Parliamentarians those of the second. Nevertheless, Arthur, though no longer the hero that Alfred had become, was allowed to survive, shorn of much of his setting. Not only did Dryden, the Catholic, think of making him the subject of a long poem, but Blackmore the Whig actually did so, giving him the semblance of William III.

The most interesting literary result of this ousting of Briton by Saxon occurs in Milton. Having written on this in my *Studies in Milton*, I shall not go into detail but merely remind you that Milton was open to all the changes just recorded. In his poem *At A Vacation Exercise*, written at the age of twenty, there is a lovely passage about the rivers of England full of references to the matter of Geoffrey of Monmouth and connecting it with recent sovereigns. (*Rivers* in the first line is the name of an undergraduate, one of the players in the scholastic masque Milton is presenting.)

> *Rivers, arise: whether thou be the son*
> *Of utmost Tweed or Ouse or gulfy Don*
> *Or Trent, who like some earth-born giant spreads*
> *His thirty arms along th'indented meads,*
> *Or sullen Mole, that runneth underneath,*
> *Or Severn swift, guilty of maiden's death,*
> *Or rocky Avon or of sedgy Lee*
> *Or coaly Tyne or ancient hallowed Dee*
> *Or Humber loud, that keeps the Scythian's name*
> *Or Medway smooth or royal-towered Thame.*

The cumulative significance of some of these references is undoubted. The maiden of whose death Severn was guilty is Sabrina, daughter of Locrine, himself son of Brutus, mythical founder of the British nation; while the previous reference to the earth-born giant suggests the giant inhabitants found by Brutus and Corineus in Albion. The Dee is hallowed because frequented by the Druids. Humber received its name from the Scythian invader,

Humber, in the time of Brutus's sons. Finally, the Thames is called royal-towered not only to praise the palaces at Westminster, Hampton, and Windsor but to bring their royal residents into connection with the complex of early legend that culminated in Arthur. Later Milton contemplated an epic on Arthur. But, after the civil war had begun, he wondered whether Alfred would provide a good subject, and of Arthur we hear no more except in the *History of Britain*, where Milton questions his historicity.

I come now to the total myth of liberty as crystalised in the eighteenth century. There may be differences of detail here and there, but the outline that follows gives it approximately. Liberty first began among certain primitive peoples, usually pastoral. Among the simple, patriarchal nomads of the east, among the Goths and Scythians, in spite of a state of ignorance and violence, such government as there was allowed greater freedom to the individual than did the great empires that arose out of the primitive state. William Temple in his *Essay on Heroic Virtue*, repeating ideas already existing in the seventeenth century, said that the Goths and Scythians were barbarically careless of their own and other peoples' lives, utterly brave, but that politically they were democratic compared with the tyrannies of Egypt, late Rome, and Turkey, where military dictatorships, the most tyrannical of all forms of government, were frequent. In particular, the north bred men of exceptional physical vigour, a vigour more likely to lead men to resist oppression than was the greater physical languor of the south. From her primitive home among shepherds and nomads it was agreed that Liberty, nearly always personified, somehow got transferred to Greece, there to flourish greatly. It was not necessary to explain how the transfer was engineered. Thomas Blackwell, in a strange book called *An Enquiry into the Life and Writings of Homer* (1735), stated that Homer lived in a hardy age, in the beginnings of liberty, so presumably within reach of primitive pastoralism, but in a temperate zone on the coast of Asia Minor which encouraged "a fine perception and a proportioned eloquence". In that favoured spot "he might view cities blessed with peace, spirited by liberty, flourishing in trade, and increasing in wealth". Blackwell here grafts onto Homer the orthodox Whig notion that trade and liberty went hand in hand. But of course it was at Athens that Liberty had her favourite home, and particularly among the orators there, who were allowed the utmost freedom of speech. From Greece Liberty spread to Rome, on one queer theory through the agency of the philosopher Pythagoras, who migrated from the Greek coast of Asia Minor to the Greek cities of southern Italy. Anyhow Liberty flourished in Republican Rome after she had been expelled from Greece when Philip of Macedon defeated Athens at the Battle of Chaeronea. And when Lord Chesterfield wrote to his son that the history of free Rome was the most instructive of all stretches of history as providing the greatest examples of virtue, wisdom, and courage he represented Whig orthodoxy faithfully. Cicero was the last and greatest of the free orators, and Rome, though powerful under Augustus, had lost her ancient liberty and ancient virtue. When the Goths broke into the decadent and enslaved Roman Empire they were purely destructive, and the myth forgets for the time being their primitive brand of freedom. Moreover, they allowed themselves to be converted to a form of Christianity far gone in decadence from its pristine purity and grossly corrupted by monkish superstition; so that the word Gothic became purely pejorative. There followed about a thousand years of Gothic and monkish gloom, during which Liberty had to retire to her home in Heaven to await better days. Those days began when the Italians grew aware of classical antiquity, whether through works of art or works of literature. Through that awareness certain cities became the home of the goddess. Pre-eminent among these was the republic of Venice, where liberty flourished long after it had been suppressed in Florence and Pisa and Siena. When most of the cities of north Italy lost their freedom, Liberty decided to move northward, where she found a most congenial home in Switzerland and more dubious ones in some of the Germanic towns. Thus on the Continent she survived precariously, and it was reserved for the favoured island of Britain to bring her into full prominence.

Coming to British history, the myth has to hark back, for Britain's case differed somewhat from the continental. Whereas on the Continent Liberty had disappeared utterly for a thousand years, traces of liberty survived in Britain throughout this unhappy span. The reason was that among primitive races, all of whom had some glimmers of the light of liberty, the Britons and the Saxons had the largest share. British resistance to the Roman invaders, typified in the heroism of Boadicea, showed that they were freedom-loving. Among the Gothic races the Saxons were pre-eminent in preserving and improving the common tradition of democratic government. According to Sir William Temple the constitution of all the Gothic peoples consisted of "a king or prince who is sovereign both in peace and war, of an assembly of barons, whom he uses as his council, and another of commons, who are representative of all that are possessed of free lands, whom the prince assembles and consults with upon the occasions and affairs of the greatest and common concern to the nation". While the Goths who invaded the Roman Empire forgot their primitive free constitution, the Saxons with their operant Witanagemot preserved and fostered it. Thus it was not surprising that in spite of the invasions and the tyrannic rule of William the Conqueror freedom was always liable to break out. The big break-out was the forcing of King John to sign Magna Charta and its subsequent confirmation by Henry III. Hume in his *History of England* wrote of this confirmation as follows:

*Thus, these famous charters were brought very nearly to the shape in which they have ever since stood; and they were, during many generations, the darling of the whole English nation and esteemed the most sacred rampart to national liberty and independence. As they secured the rights of all orders of men, they were regarded with a jealous eye by all and became the basis, in a manner, of the English monarchy [see frontispiece of* Little Arthur's History] *and a kind of original contract, which both limited the authority of the king and ensured the conditional allegiance of his subjects. Though often violated, they were still claimed and recalled by the nobility and people; and as no precedents were supposed valid that infringed them, they rather acquired than lost authority from the frequent attempts, made against them in several ages by regal and arbitrary power.*

For the next stage of freedom we have to go abroad: to Luther and the Reformation. It was Luther who first broke monkish tyranny, though it was not his country that most used the break to promote liberty. It needed the defeat of the Spanish Armada by England to consolidate the gains that Luther's revolt had made possible. There were options about how you took the English civil war of the seventeenth century, but the myth carefully avoided both extremes and decided to look on that war as presenting problems not solved till the glorious events of 1688.

That opinion, apart from the Jacobites', accepted this estimate of the 1689 settlement, is beyond doubt. Indeed the evidence is overwhelming. Here is typical evidence from early in the century, a passage from *A Sermon preached at the Assizes at Hartford* (1708) by Bishop Benjamin Hoadley:

> *This great island is one kingdom, governed after the most desirable manner and the least liable to great evils. True liberty flourishes; property is securely possessed; and all enjoy the freedom of worshipping God as their consciences direct; and a prospect of a long enjoyment of all these happinesses is afforded us by the distant view of succeeding princes, who, we may hope, will learn from the present example to account it their chief glory to preserve these blessings, and their own greatest happiness to make their people happy. And need I tell you to what it is that we owe these singular and invaluable happinesses? Is it not too plain to need any proof that we owe them all entirely to the late revolution and those principles upon which it was founded?*

Voltaire, rather later in the century (his *Lettres Philo-*

*sophiques* were first published in 1734), writing his letter on the English Parliament, said that the English nation was the only one that had succeeded in curbing its king by resisting him and in establishing the happy state where he has every power to do good, while his hands are tied should he attempt to do ill, where the nobles having no vassals are not insolent, and where the people share in the government without riot. Late in the century Joseph Priestley, Unitarian minister, wrote in his *Lectures on History*:

> *The most important period of our history is that of the revolution under King William. Then it was that our constitution, after many fluctuations and frequent struggles for power by the different members of it . . . was finally settled. A revolution so remarkable and attended with such happy consequences has perhaps no parallel in the history of the world.*

It is pointless to quote more passages to the same effect.

The myth includes three large general principles: first that, as hinted by Blackwell in his book on Homer, freedom encourages commerce, and commerce freedom; second, that the arts flourish most in a free society; and last that the world is getting better. To illustrate the first and second I need not go to anything less well known than Thomson's *Rule, Britannia!* It is because liberty flourishes in Britain, because Britons never will be slaves, that

> *To thee belongs the rural reign;*
>   *Thy cities shall with commerce shine;*
> *All thine shall be the subject main,*
>   *And every shore it circles thine,*

where the last line means not that Britain will annex the total coastline of the world but that she will see to it through her sea-power that she can trade freely on every coast. And Thomson goes on to the second principle when he writes:

*The Muses, still with freedom found,*
*Shall to thy happy isle repair.*

Some writers admit that there are exceptions to this general rule, that the arts have in fact sometimes flourished under an absolute monarch. But here is a passage that will have none of this; again from Blackwell's strange book on Homer. Referring to the present literatures of France and Spain where of old the arts flourished he wrote:

*How barren now in real literature! How distorted the little they produce! . . . Instead of those bold pictures of men and things in the present age, they must content themselves with licking up scraps of monkish history and collecting the legends of the Saints; or if they venture to reason, it must be upon distant facts and general principles, remote from their own times, without daring to hint a parallel or make the smallest application. Such is their state; while we, with joy, may view our native isle, the happy instance of the connexion of Liberty and Learning. We find our language masculine and noble; of vast extent and capable of greater variety of style and character than any modern tongue. We see our arts improving, our sciences advancing, life understood, and the whole animated with a spirit so generous and free as gives the truest proof of the happiness of our constitution.*

The last sentence will serve to show how the eighteenth-century myth of liberty included the doctrine of progress.

If the Tudor and Augustan myths of national history differed in not making the same events mythical, the Augustan myth of total history differed from the medieval by including this doctrine of progress. The Middle Ages aspired to be all-inclusive but were unaware of any principle of evolution. The Augustan notion of history was crudely selective, by modern historical standards ridiculous, but it postulated a process and a development and sought to connect past, present, and future.

It is easy to mock at the whole myth with its staggering omissions and its travesties of fact; and with redoubled readiness after Herbert Butterfield put us on our guard against the Whig interpretation of history. But we must not allow his brilliance to prevent our seeing that the myth of liberty meant something in its day. Nothing could be more open than parts of it to the error he exposes of interpreting past events through present prejudices. But the most important element of all was so recent that it escapes his strictures. And this was the revolution of 1688; and we must beware of ridiculing or of belittling the emotions this aroused in the majority of men in the years that followed it. They knew from what it had saved them; and their pride in its bloodlessness deserves nothing but praise. In reviewing the myth we should temper our mirth by heeding what G. M. Trevelyan said about the 1689 settlement in his *History of England*.

*The settlement of 1689 stood the test of time. It led not only to a new and wider liberty than had ever before been known in*

*Britain, but to a renewed vigour and efficiency in the body politic and in the government of the Empire. The long and enervating rivalry of Crown and Parliament gave place to co-operation between the two powers, with Parliament the leading partner. From the external weakness that had characterized England in the Seventeenth Century the country rose through the successive eras of Marlborough, Walpole, and Chatham to the acknowledged leadership of the world, in arms, colonies, and commerce, in political and religious freedom and intellectual vigour.*

*The men of 1689 were not heroes. Few of them were even honest men. But they were very clever men, and, taught by bitter experience, they behaved at this supreme crisis as very clever men do not always behave, with sense and moderation. It was the gravity of the national danger in the first months of 1689, with France in arms against us, Scotland divided and Ireland lost, that induced Whigs and Tories in the Convention Parliament to make that famous compromise between their conflicting principles and factions, which we call the Revolution Settlement. It remained the solid foundation of English institutions in Church and State, almost without change until the era of the Reform Bill.*

If this is so and if the other parts of the myth satisfied the men of the eighteenth century as leading worthily up to the supreme event, it follows that the total myth had the initial potentiality of inspiring great literature. It remains to inquire how far that potentiality was realised.

The most ambitious attempt to embody the myth in verse was Thomson's *Liberty*. (And let me add at this point that for a brief contemporary compendium of the myth you cannot do better than go to the table of contents prefixed to the first four books of the poem, and second that the best place to find information about its nature and history is A. D. McKillop's *Background of Thomson's "Liberty"*, a work to which I am greatly indebted throughout this section.) *Liberty* is a poem in five books, in which the poet, like Gibbon conceiving the notion of writing the *Decline and Fall*, meditates among the ruins of Rome until

> *the fair majestic form*
> *Of Liberty appeared. Not, as of old,*
> *Extended in her hand the cap and rod*
> *Whose slave-enlarging touch gave double life;*
> *But her bright temples bound with British oak,*
> *And naval honours nodded on her brow.*

Liberty proceeds to tell the poet that the fragments of antiquity that lie around are survivals from the earlier days of Roman freedom and to enlarge on the present ravages caused by the monster, Oppression. And she draws the moral that Britain must preserve her present happiness, for, with her grimmer climate, she will, if she lapses into sloth and yields to Oppression, suffer an even worse fate than modern Italy. The poet then asks for further enlightenment, and Liberty, consenting, fills the rest of the poem by recounting the history of her spirit throughout the ages, its culmination in the 1689 Settlement, and lastly the means by which it may be fostered.

It is common to find the motive of *Liberty* in the continental tour which Thomson made as tutor to Charles Talbot. But since this tour did not include Greece, which figures largely in the poem, and since all his material was common property, it is wiser to look for a motive elsewhere. When Thomson began *Liberty* he had already collected the different *Seasons* into a single volume and appeared to have achieved a successful long poem; and at least he had achieved a popular one. That poem had much in common with the *Georgics* of Virgil; and the Virgilian analogy, doubtless impressed on him by admiring friends, and especially Lord Lyttelton, may have tempted him to something more ambitious corresponding to the *Aeneid*. For such an epic aspiration he chose a fitting subject, something dear to the hearts of a large body of men, but the *Seasons* should have already made clear to him that he was not capable of a genuine long poem. The *Seasons* may still be read with pleasure for the descriptive passages, for its keen and delicate observation of detail, and for the accompanying delicacy of sound, but the descriptions and the homiletic passages that link them do not add up to a coherent whole. We get a vague impression that Thomson was an amiable man, not that he was possessed by a great subject. In *Liberty* he knows that his subject is great and he sticks to it, but, alas, all too grimly and tautologically. He gives, in remorselessly direct presentation, instance after instance of men or countries that liberty has inspired, slightly diversified by instances of oppression and slavery. There is no letting up, and the only relief from homiletic solemnity are the passages of description. Although *Liberty* did not fall so flat in its own day as is popularly supposed, there is little chance of the quickly reached verdict of unreadableness being reversed.

All the same *Liberty* has not had its due. It has many beautiful passages and some noble ones; like Shelley's *Revolt of Islam* it is the repository of fine things, embedded in dullness and unjustly forgotten. There are many passages as good as the best things in the *Seasons* and of the same kind, like the picture of the desolate Roman *campagna* near the beginning, or this passage describing the Greek invention of landscape-painting:

> *There gaily broke the sun-illumined cloud;*
> *The lessening prospect and the mountain blue*
> *Vanished in air; the precipice frowned dire;*
> *White down the rock the rushing torrent dashed;*
> *The sun shone trembling o'er the distant main;*
> *The tempest foamed immense; the driving storm*
> *Saddened the skies, and, from the doubling gloom,*
> *On the scathed oak the ragged lightning fell;*
> *In closing shades, and where the current strays,*
> *With peace and love and innocence around,*
> *Piped the lone shepherd to the feeding flock.*

This is a delicate and sensitive rendering of the types of landscape dear to the contemporary artist, the broken lines and staccato rhythms of the scenes of storm issuing into the leisurely rhythms of the quiet pastoral. But Thomson can be more startling, as in this account, narrated by Liberty personified, of Greece corrupted by Persian gold and subdued by Philip of Macedon:

> *Thus, tame, submitted to the victor's yoke,*
> *Greece, once the gay, the turbulent, the bold;*
> *For every grace and muse and science born;*
> *With arts of war, of government elate;*
> *Whom I myself could scarcely rule: and thus*
> *The Persian fetters, that enthralled the mind,*
> *Were turned to formal and apparent chains.*

I know of no passage that could be better used to repel the charge, less common than it once was, that the eighteenth century poets were normally unable to use words in any fresh or stirring way. The thought of Greece made a fresh impact on Thomson's mind when he called her "the gay, the turbulent, the bold, Whom I myself could scarcely rule"; the adjectives correspond surprisingly to fact, and it is through their being surprising that they make fact significant. If they had appeared in a less obscure context they might have taken on the proverbial quality which the very fresh statements of old truths can attain to. There is the same freshness in the "formal and apparent chains". Then at times the frigid, brassy rhetoric that is the poem's norm gives way to something more passionate and more legitimately heightened, as when at the end of the third book Liberty, lost to the world during the Dark Ages, takes the arts with her to seek refuge in a celestial home till she may visit earth once more. This is how Thomson describes this celestial home:

> In the bright regions there of purest day
> Far other scenes and palaces arise,
> Adorned profuse with other arts divine.
> All beauty here below, to them compared,
> Would, like a rose before the midday sun,
> Shrink up its blossom—like a bubble break
> The passing poor magnificence of kings.
> For there the King of Nature in full blaze
> Calls every splendour forth, and there his court
> Amid etherial powers and virtues holds—
> Angel, archangel, tutelary gods

*Of cities, nations, empires, and of worlds.*
*But sacred be the veil that kindly clouds*
*A light too keen for mortals—wraps a view*
*Too softening fair for those that here in dust*
*Must cheerful toil out their appointed years.*
*A sense of higher life would only damp*
*The schoolboy's task and spoil his playful hours.*
*Nor could the child of reason, feeble man,*
*With vigour through this infant-being drudge,*
*Did brighter worlds, their unimagined bliss*
*Disclosing, dazzle and dissolve his mind.*

Apart from this spasmodic literary merit, *Liberty* is highly interesting in giving the best summary of the historical myth that is the subject of this section. Bits of the myth occur in Addison and Shaftesbury, and of course for general principles on politics, property, and trade there was Locke in the background. But to find the total myth set out in prose you have to go to writers far more voluminous than Thomson, and conspicuously to two French authors. First there is Rollin, whose *Histoire Ancienne* (recommended by Chesterfield to his son) Mckillop describes as a "naïve and popular presentation of ancient history in terms of civic virtue and republicanism, kept by countless Whigs and Liberals in Britain and America in their libraries and schools to demonstrate the political and moral lessons taught by the ancient world". Second there is the French Huguenot historian, Rapin de Thoyras, whose *History of England*, very widely read, contains the English portion of the Whig myth. Both writers are ample; and anyone interested in no more than the outlines of the myth will find them more conveniently in Thomson's *Liberty* than in any other place I know of.

The best-known poem embodying the myth of liberty is Collins's *Ode to Liberty*. It is a queer, turgid affair, plainly seeking to be Pindaric through its turgidity and through the number and difficulty of its allusions, but it is also a work of genius, of a man with an uncommon imagination and an uncommon command of the music of words. Ignoring initially the primitive part of the myth, it begins abruptly with the freedom-loving youths of Sparta and with the praise of Harmodius and Aristogiton, who brought freedom to Athens by killing the tyrant Pisistratus. It commemorates Rome only in deploring the loss of the freedom she once enjoyed; and through the common rhetorical device of the poet's saying that he will *not* tell this and that.

> *No, Freedom, no, I will not tell,*
> *How Rome before thy weeping face,*
> *With heaviest sounds, a giant-statue, fell,*
> *Pushed by a wild and artless race*
> *From off its wide, ambitious base,*
> *When Time his northern sons of spoil awoke,*
> *    And all the blended work of strength and grace,*
> *    With many a rude repeated stroke*
> *And many a barb'rous yell, to thousand fragments broke.*

Collins then repeats the part of the myth that attributed the first revival of freedom in Europe to the appreciation of any fragments of classical antiquity that survived the barbarian invasions.

> *Yet ev'n, whene'er the least appeared,*
> *Th'admiring world thy hand revered;*

*Still midst the scattered states around*
*Some remnants of her strength were found:*
*They saw by what escaped the storm*
*How wondrous rose her perfect form;*
*How in the great, the laboured whole*
*Each mighty master poured his soul.*

And there follows a list of Italian cities where freedom and
the arts flourished, Venice being pre-eminent among them.
Collins next is perfectly correct in making Liberty migrate
from Italy northward across the Alps and alludes to the
legend of Tell's freeing Switzerland from the Austrian yoke.

*Ah no! more pleased thy haunts I seek*
*On wild Helvetia's mountains bleak,*
*Where, when the favoured of thy choice,*
*The daring archer, heard thy voice,*
*Forth from his eyrie roused in dread,*
*The ravening eagle northward fled.*

Holland comes next, leading to the climax in Britain,
whose praises occupy the rest, that is one half, of the ode.
In this climax comes, first, a strange and sublime passage
(claimed by Collins in a footnote to treat a subject un-
attempted in poetry before) describing how Britain, once
joined to the Continent, was loosened from it in a furious
storm and, to Freedom's great benefit, became an island.
In cloudy grandiosity Collins then refers to the freedom
endemic in the primitive folk of Britain by picturing her
shrine in some green depth of the island.

*There oft the painted native's feet*
*Were wont thy form celestial meet;*
*Though now with hopeless toil we trace*
*Time's backward rolls to find its place.*

The shrine was destroyed, either by the Danes or the Romans, but the Platonic Idea of it, the model, exists in heaven.

> *There happier than in islands blessed*
> *Or bowers by spring or Hebe dressed*
> *The chiefs who fill our Albion's story*
> *In warlike weeds, retired in glory,*
> *Hear their consorted Druids sing*
> *Their triumphs to th'immortal string.*

The ode ends with a description of the architecture of the heavenly shrine.

> *In Gothic pride it seems to rise,*
> *Yet Graecia's graceful orders join*
> *Majestic through the mixed design;*

which is Collins's allegorical way of saying that the principle of liberty combines the primitivism of the Goths with the republicanism of Greece and Rome: an essential part of the liberty myth. Collins does not deal with English history but calls on the heroes of that history to persuade the goddess, Concord, to visit "Britain's ravaged shore", referring, as he does elsewhere in his poems, to the Jacobite war of 1745.

Confined as he is to an ode, Collins has to omit parts of the myth, but it is quite plain that he was acquainted with the whole and owed his inspiration to it.

By far the most important work of literature inspired by the myth of liberty is Gibbon's *Decline and Fall of the Roman Empire*. I will only summarise my views, since I have given them in my book on the English epic. What I assert is that Gibbon's history is not simply a record of an important series of events; at bottom it is an objectifica-

tion in artistic form of certain principles in which he
fervently believed. It is of course much more; but you
will never do the great work justice unless you see on
what it is ultimately based. Gibbon was of course interested in the late Roman empire for all the variety and
excitement its history offered. But that this kind of
interest was not paramount in deciding his choice is
evident from his having considered other topics: first the
life of some great man, second the history of Swiss
freedom, and last the history of Florence under the
Medici. What is also to the point here is that the rise of
the Swiss, the loss of freedom in Florence through the
rule of the Medici, and the decline and fall of the Roman
empire were all organic parts of the total myth. Gibbon
contemplated his writing of history as the epic poet
contemplates the making of his long poem. Both know
that selection is imperative, that they must convey the
general through the particular; and Gibbon wanted to
find the stretch of history whose course would best
express those general principles about which he felt with
such warmth. The rise of Switzerland would have suited
him well, but he felt a distaste for the crabbed German he
would have to read in going to the original authorities.
Perhaps he also perceived unconsciously that a story of
almost constant success such as the rise of Switzerland
appealed to the feelings less than the tragic decline of the
world's greatest empire. As to the Medici, the alternative subject to Switzerland, his own words are very
much to the present point:

> *I have another subject in view, which is the contrast of the*
> *former history: the one a poor, warlike, virtuous republic,*

*which emerges into glory and freedom; the other a common-wealth, soft, opulent, and corrupt; which by just degrees is precipitated from the abuse to the loss of her liberty. Both lessons are, perhaps, equally instructive.*

And he gives a list of the varied turns of events in Florence under the Medici until "the genius of Freedom reluctantly yielded to the arms of Charles V and the policy of Cosmo". We may conjecture that the events of a single city did not satisfy the scope of his ambitions. But neither he nor we can really know the mixture of motives that possessed him at the famous moment when at Rome, on the 15th of October 1764, as he sat musing amidst the ruins of the Capitol, while the barefooted friars were singing vespers in the temple of Jupiter, the idea of writing the decline and fall of the city first started to his mind. What we can be certain of is that he made his choice, as he thought he might choose the Medici, in order to be "instructive", in other words in order to present in action the myth of liberty, to which beyond all doubt he was entirely loyal.

Where Gibbon most differed from other expounders was in his choosing as his chief theme those dark ages that they could not bear to dwell on. Collins in his ode said he would *not* tell of the Gothic destruction of the Roman achievement. Gibbon is fascinated by all the details and the intricacy of the monkish superstition that was part of the myth but was generally thought too painful a theme to be studied closely. And contrariwise Gibbon included either as appendices to his theme or through incidental reference those parts of the myth that had received most attention from other writers. For instance, he enlarges on

the greatness of free republican Rome in his chapters on
the Roman army and the legal code of Justinian; while at
the other extreme he refers obliquely to the restriction of
the monarchy in evil (which Voltaire had praised as part
of the 1689 Settlement) in describing the opposite state
of things under the Roman Empire. The Antonine
emperors, he says,

> *must often have recollected the instability of a happiness which
> depended on the character of a single man. The fatal moment
> was perhaps approaching, when some licentious youth, or some
> jealous tyrant, would abuse, to the destruction, that absolute
> power which they had exerted for the benefit of their people.*

And in his account, near the end of his history, of Rienzi's
attempt, supported by Petrarch, to revive the order and
the spirit of ancient Rome, Gibbon is citing one of those
fragments of freedom to which Collins referred as warm-
ing men's hearts after the Dark Ages and in anticipation
of its future flowering in northern Europe. Gibbon
even refers directly to the enlightenment of the age
of Newton, as in this passage about the appearance of
Halley's comet in the age of Justinian. Talking of its
various appearances, he writes:

> *The seventh phaenomenon, of one thousand six hundred and
> eighty, was presented to the eyes of an enlightened age. The
> philosophy of Bayle dispelled a prejudice which Milton's muse
> had so recently adorned, that the comet "from its horrid hair
> shakes pestilence and war". Its road in the heavens was
> observed with exquisite skill by Flamsteed and Cassini; and the
> mathematical science of Bernouilli, Newton, and Halley, in-
> vestigated the laws of its revolutions. At the eighth period, in*

*the year two thousand three hundred and fifty-five, their calculations may perhaps be verified by the astronomers of some future capital in the Siberian or American wilderness.*

All these instances go to show first that Gibbon accepted the total myth and second that, as said before, his technique in presenting it was the selective, retrospective, and prophetic one of the epic poet.

The last quotation may serve to illustrate two other features of the *Decline and Fall*: first the belief in progress and second the passion that informs it. I have said little so far about progress, because it was another myth of the age, in its own right; but that it contributed to the myth of liberty is undoubted. There is something peculiarly impressive about the way Gibbon speaks about progress. He believes in it in spite of his scepticism and of his unsleeping awareness of human frailty. And that gives his references to it a weight that similar references by the more easily optimistic lack. They are more weighty than for instance this fine passage from the work of Joseph Priestley already referred to in this section:

*Let the person who would trace the conduct of Divine Providence attend to every advantage which the present age enjoys above ancient times and see whether he cannot perceive marks of things being in a progress towards a state of greater perfection. Let him particularly attend to every event which contributes to the propagation of religious knowledge; and, lastly, let him carefully observe all the evils which mankind complain of and consider whether they be not either remedies of greater evils, or, supposing the general constitution of things unalterable, the necessary means of introducing a greater degree of happiness than could have been brought about by any other means. . . .*

*That the state of the world at present, and particularly the state of Europe, is vastly preferable to what it was in any former period, is evident from the very first view of things. A thousand circumstances show how inferior the ancients were to the moderns in religious knowledge, in science in general, in government, in laws, both the laws of nations and those of particular states, in arts, in commerce, in the conveniences of life, in manners, and in consequence of all these in happiness.*

Where Gibbon's passage on Halley's comet surpasses this one of Priestley is in its stronger and more securely based emotion. It gives us confidence by its precise and lavish detail; it appeals to our emotions by its cunning reference to a great place in poetry, by its bidding our imaginations roam into the future, and by a heightening of rhythm which it is beyond my skill to analyse. It is penetrated by that concern with man's destiny which was Gibbon's demon, his good demon that kept him to his task and which made all the intricate detail of that task acceptable, miraculously, to the attention of his reader. I will confirm these assertions by quoting another passage both dealing with progress and bearing the impression of passion even more plainly. It has to do not with the kind of progress pictured through the probable growth of civilisation between the years 1680 and 2355 but with the securing of certain basic goods that will not be affected by those setbacks which Gibbon recognised as only too likely to afflict the slow and hesitant advance of mankind and from which progress may yet be resumed after evil days:

*Fortunately for mankind, the more useful, or at least, more necessary arts, can be performed without superior talents. . . .*

*Each village, each family, each individual, must always possess both ability and inclination, to perpetuate the use of fire and of metals; the propagation and service of domestic animals; the methods of hunting and fishing; the rudiments of navigation; the imperfect cultivation of corn or other nutritive grain; and the simple practice of the mechanic trades. Private genius and public industry may be extirpated; but these hardy plants survive the tempest and strike an everlasting root into the most unfavourable soil. The splendid days of Augustus and Trajan were eclipsed by a cloud of ignorance; and the Barbarians subverted the laws and palaces of Rome. But the scythe, the invention or emblem of Saturn, still continued to mow the harvests of Italy; and the human feasts of the Laestrygons have never been renewed on the coast of Campania.*

This passage has the qualities of the previous one quoted: the reassurance given by the abundant detail and the bidding of the reader's imagination to roam, this time not forward but backward to days when there were still cannibals in Europe; but the rhythms are even more heightened, betraying an even intenser passion. It is a queer comparison, but his passage reminds me of nothing so much both in basic sentiment and in fervour as of the last lines of Shelley's *Prometheus Unbound*, when the poet asks by what means liberty, once lost, can be regained. The answer is hope, forgiveness, defiance of absolute power, love, endurance, stedfastness. In this passage Shelley descends from his ecstatic vision of a redeemed universe to the sober thought that a happy state of things on earth is liable to mutability; in the other passage Gibbon, the man of the world, the realist, allows himself the hope that on a balance the world is getting better and that there is a point beneath which it will not sink and from which it will rise. From their different beginnings the two authors, apparently so opposed in temperament, have reached pretty much the same position. Gibbon would have accepted Shelley's list of remedial virtues, even love; for did he not end his penultimate chapter, where he finishes with the affairs of the Catholic Church, with the words, "For myself, it is my wish to depart in charity with all mankind, nor am I willing, in these last moments, to offend even the pope and clergy of Rome"? Of course he would have disliked the excesses of Shelley's method of statement. "To forgive wrongs darker than death or night", that would be altogether too extreme and too little specified; "to hope till hope creates, From its own wreck the thing it contemplates" would be altogether too fanciful. But do not suppose that such an inability to appreciate implies any lack of feeling. Hogg in his life of Shelley records Shelley's excitement when he got hold of a new book which he thought might enlighten him: his voracity in reading it and his forgetfulness of mealtimes. Gibbon in his autobiography wrote of himself as follows:

> *In the summer of 1751 I accompanied my father on a visit to Mr Hoare's, in Wiltshire; but I was less delighted with the beauties of Stourhead than with discovering in the library a common book, the* Continuation of Echard's Roman History. . . . *To me the reigns of the successors of Constantine were absolutely new; and I was immersed in the passage of the Goths over the Danube, when the summons of the dinner bell reluctantly dragged me from my intellectual feast.*

Gibbon obeyed the summons to dinner not because he

*felt* less keenly than Shelley but only because of his loyalty to the rigid social demands of the eighteenth century.

The *Decline and Fall* is so rich, so sophisticated, so wise that it seems unfair to link it to the crudities that most forms of the myth of Liberty issued into. I had rather say that it is unfair to the myth not to give it credit for the one major work of art of which it was the animating principle.

# INDEX

*Acts of Pilate*, see *Nicodemus, Gospel of*

Alfred, King, supplants Arthur, 110

André of Toulouse, Poet Laureate to Henry VII, 49, 51, 53

Angelico, Fra, 23

Angels, nine orders of, 25

Aquinas, 24

Arnold, Matthew, 17

Arthur, King, 48, 52, 110, 114
  ceases to be national figure, 110-12

Arthur, Prince, son of Henry VII, 48

Avery, Myrtilla, edition of Exultet Rolls, 23

Battle of the Bulge, mythical significance of, 12

Benlowes, Edward, *Theophila*, 80-2

Bernard, Saint, version of theme of Four Daughters of God, 42

Bernardus Andreas, see André of Toulouse

Blackwell, Thomas, *Enquiry into Life and Writings of Homer*, 115, 119-20

Blake, William, *Holy Thursday*, 15-17

Bosworth, Battle of, 53 110

Brinkley, R. F., 112

Brutus, ancestor of British kings, 48-9, 114

Bunyan, John, *Holy War*, 70, *Pilgrim's Progress*, 69

Burns, Robert, *Holy Willie's Prayer*, 69

Butterfield, Herbert, 121

Cadwallader, 48-9

Callcott, Lady, 109
  *Little Arthur's History of England*, 108-11

Capgrave, chronicler, 25-6

Casimir, see Sarbiewski

Catherine de Valois, wife of Henry V, 46, 50-1

Chaucer, *Sir Thopas*, 36

Chester Plays, 36-7

Collins, William, *Ode to Liberty*, 128-30, 133

Coventry Plays, 36-7

Cowper, William, *Retirement*, 102-7

*Cursor Mundi*, 34-6

Cyprus, mythology of Republic of, 13

Dante, 24

Dee, John, mathematician, 52

139

Defoe, Daniel, *Robinson Crusoe*, 96-101
Devils, nine orders of, 25
Dickens, *Oliver Twist*, 16-17
*Pickwick Papers*, 17
Donne, John, 85
*Third Satire*, 69
Drayton, Michael, *England's Heroical Epistles*, 51-2

Edward IV, 25
Eliot, T. S.
*Family Reunion*, 62
*Murder in the Cathedral*, 63
Elizabeth, Yorkist heiress, 55
Elizabeth I, 56-7, 111
Exultet Rolls, 22-3

Fairfax, Lord, Parliamentary General, 82-3
Fan Chung-Yen, *On the Frontier*, 13-15, 44
Fletcher, John, playwright, 63
Foakes, R. A., 64
Ford, John, *'Tis Pity She's a Whore*, 68-9
Four Daughters of God, medieval theme of, 41-3

General Strike, mythical significance of, 13

Gentility, nine orders of, 25
Geoffrey of Monmouth, *Historia Regum Britanniae*, 48-9, 110, 112-13
Gibbon, Edward, *Decline and Fall of Roman Empire*, 123, 130-8
Goldsmith, Oliver, *History of England*, 111
Grant, Douglas, 94
Greenlaw, E., *Studies in Spenser's Historical Allegory*, 50

Hall, Edward, chronicler, 54, 57, 61, 63
Haller, William, *Rise of Puritanism*, 69
Heine, *Die Lorelei*, indispensable as myth, 12-13
Henry IV, 25
Henry VI, 47, 54
Henry VII, 47-9, 53-5
Henry VIII, 53, 55-6, 63
Herbert, George, 85
Hoadley, Benjamin, 118
Holkham Hall, 94
Homily, *Against Disobedience*, 56
Horace, on Retirement, 74-76
Hume, David, *History of England*, 117
Insurrections, Catholic, 56-7

James, Montague, *Apocryphal New Testament*, 21, 26
Joan of Arc, 110-11
*Justa Edwardo King*, 29

King's College Chapel, windows in, 19-20, 24-5, 29
Kossovo, ballads on Battle of, 78

Langland, *Piers Plowman*, 31
    treatment of Harrowing of Hell in, 42-4
Lawrence, D. H., *Plumed Serpent*, 73-4
Llewelyn, royal Welsh house of, 51, 112
Lucretius, on Retirement, 74-5, 85
Luther, Martin, as promoter of liberty, 118

McKillop, A. D., 123, 127
Magna Charta, 109-12, 117
Mall, Edward, 32
Mattingly, Garrett, on Spanish Armada, 12
Marvell, Andrew, *The Garden*, 82-4
Meres, F., *Palladis Tamia*, 50
Milton, John, 70-1, 84, 113-14

*Mirror for Magistrates*, 45
Monkhouse Museum, 13
Myth
    as inspiring literature, 15
    literature having the function of, 15, 17-18
    meaning of in this book, 9-13
    practical effect of, 17-18, 28, 93

Newton, Sir Isaac, 93-4
*Nicodemus, Gospel of*, 20-23, 34-6, 41-2, 44
    Anglo-Saxon version, 31
    medieval version, 34
    put on Index by Council of Trent, 29
Norris, John, of Bemerton, 85-7, 91
*Northern Passion*, theme of Harrowing of Hell in, 33-4

Ovid, *Art of Love*, 107

Pearson, John, *Exposition of the Creed*, 29-31
Plutarch, *Lives*, 45
Pollard, A. W., *English Miracle Plays*, 32
Pomfret, John, 87, 90-1
Pope, Alexander, 102, 105
Priestley, Joseph, 119
Puritanism, 69-70

Rapin de Thoyras, *History of England*, 127

Ray, John, *Wisdom of God manifested in the Works of Creation*, 92-3, 95, 103

Redemption, doctrine of, 27-8, 41

Richard II, 54

Richard III, 53, 55, 63

Rollin, *Histoire Ancienne*, 127

Rossiter, A. P., on medieval dramatic cycles, 35

Røstvig, Maren-Sophie, on Retirement, 72, 79, 85, 93-5, 102

Rowse, A. L., 52

St. Paul's Cathedral, mythical significance of, 11

Sarbiewski, Mathias Casimir, 75-9, 81, 91

Self-help, as Victorian myth, 18

Shakespeare, William, 56-65

    *Coriolanus*, 62

    *Hamlet*, 63

    *Henry IV*, 61

    *Henry V*, 62

    *Henry VI*, 57-9, 67

    *Henry VIII*, 63-5

    *Richard II*, 61, 65

    *Richard III*, 53, 57-61, 65

Shelley, P. B.

    *Prometheus Unbound*, 136-8

*Revolt of Islam*, 124

Sidney, Sir Philip, *Arcadia*, 67

Sorel, Georges, *Reflexions on Violence*, 13

Southey, Robert, 111

Spanish Armada, mythical significance of, 12

*Spectator*, 91, 95

Speirs, John, on Harrowing of Hell, 28

Spenser, Edmund

    *Colin Clout*, 74

    *Fairy Queen*, 49

Switzer, Stephen, horticulturalist, 96

Temple, William, *Essay on Heroic Virtue*, 114, 116

Thomson, James

    *Liberty*, 122-8

    *Rule, Britannia!*, 119-20

    *Sacred to the Memory of Sir Isaac Newton*, 93

    *Seasons*, 93-4, 102, 124-125

Tintoretto, 23

Trent, Council of, 29

Trevelyan, G. M., 121-2

Tudor, Owen, 46, 51

Vaughan, Henry, 75-7, 79, 90, 103

Vickey, cartoonist, 11

Virgil, *Georgics*, 74, 124

Voltaire, *Lettres Philosophiques*, 118-19, 133

Wakefield Plays, 36-8

Warner, *Albion's England*, 50-1, 54

*Epitome of whole History of England*, 54-5

Watts, Doctor, 91

Wigan, mythical significance of

Winchelsea, Anne, Countess of, 87-90

Witanagemot, 117

Wyatt, Sir Thomas, 74

York Plays, 36

play on Harrowing of Hell, 38, 41, 44, 60